No One Told Me I Could Cry

by
Connie Nykiel R.N., B.S.H.A., C.P.C.E.

Life Cycle Books Ltd.
Lewiston, NY • Toronto, ON

All scripture citations are from the Good News Bible: The Bible in Today's English Version (1979). New York: American Bible Society.

All names, traits, and places have been changed in order to protect the young women who have shared their confidences.

Library of Congress Catalog Card Number: 95-90855
ISBN: 0-919225-19-5

Published by:
Life Cycle Books
P.O. Box 420
Lewiston, NY 14092-0420

Phone: (800) 214-5849
Fax: (888) 690-8532
e-mail: orders@lifecyclebooks.com
www.lifecyclebooks.com

Canada Office:
Life Cycle Books Ltd.
421 Nugget Ave. #8
Toronto, ON M1S 4L8

Printed in Canada

ACKNOWLEDGMENTS

So many have contributed to this book both directly and indirectly. I couldn't have done it without you. All praise and all thanksgiving to my Father in heaven for His love, protection, and blessings, Jesus my Savior, the most loving and forgiving of all hearts, and the Holy Spirit for putting the persistent thought in my mind that this book must be written as well as for His presence as it was written.

Much love and thanks to my parents, Jack and Doris Corso, for teaching me to love and respect life. Deepest appreciation goes to my husband, Tom, for his love, support, prayers, comforting words and actions, closing the office door when I needed quiet, and understanding my faraway look. Thanks to all my children, for sacrificing time that I could have spent with you.

I would like to give recognition to Vicki Thorn and Trish Shickert of the National Office of Post-Abortion Reconciliation and Healing, Ken Freeman of Last Harvest Ministries, Dr. Vincent Rue of the Institute for Pregnancy Loss and Recovery, David Reardon of the Elliot Institute, Wayne Brauning of Men's Abortion ReCovery (MARC), Jane Meyer of the Life Issues Institute, Judy McDonough of CareNet, Patty Slauson of Open Arms, and Elizabeth Verchio of Victims of Choice for their telephone time and information, but most of all for their work in the field of post-abortion recovery. Grateful thanks for the prayers of Focus on the Family, and the St. Anthony's Prayer Group in Frankfort, IL, and many thanks for the helpfulness of the Frankfort Public Library staff.

This book is dedicated to all young women
who have suffered the loss of their child through
abortion. May you read this book and be comforted.

CONTENTS

Foreword xi

Chapter 1 *Tiffany's Story* 1

Chapter 2 *A Secret Sorrow* 5

Chapter 3 *When Emotions Overflow* 9
Healthy and Unhealthy Guilt 10
Psychological Symptoms 10
Physical Symptoms 13
Emotional Symptoms 13
Anniversary Syndrome 16
When Does Post Abortion Syndrome Begin 17

Chapter 4 *What You Should Know About
Teenagers and Abortion* 19

Chapter 5 *How Abortion Affects Young Fathers* 21
Abortion Attitudes of Young Men 21
The Effects of Abortion on Young Men 22
Relationships and Abortion 24
If You and Your Baby's Mother Are No Longer Together 26

Chapter 6 *How Teenagers Deal With Abortion* 27
Why Can't I Go On This Way? I'm Doing Just Fine 29

Chapter 7 *Getting Ready to Grieve* 31

Chapter 8 *The Grief Process* 35
Denial 35
Anger 41
Bargaining 46
Depression 51
Acceptance 52
Hope 53

Chapter 9 *Forgiveness*. 55
  Forgiving God 57
  Forgiving Others 59
  Asking God to Forgive You 61
  Forgiving Yourself 63
  Asking Your Baby to Forgive You. 63

Chapter 10 *Hope and Joy* 67
  Future Plans and Goals. 67
  Celebrate by Thanking God 68

Appendix
  Where To Get Help. 69
  References 75

FOREWORD

I teach childbirth education to pregnant teenagers. My job is to prepare young parents for parenthood. This includes the possibility of parenting a baby with a birth defect or being the parent of the baby that is miscarried, stillborn, or dies soon after birth. This is the hardest class for me to teach. Young mothers don't want to talk or think about it. It is their worst fear. I usually end up telling them that if it is too painful to think about their own babies dying, then listen and learn how to help others who have lost a baby. We talk about the stages of grief, the feelings of those who are mourning, what to say and what not to say. We read poems and letters that mothers have written to their babies.

When I held this class during the fall of 1993, the girls, like all the girls in the classes before them, put their hands over their ears and said they didn't want to hear about it. Despite their protests I taught the class and before I knew it, the girls were talking about an aunt, cousin or friend who had lost a baby. They said they wished they would have known what to do and say before. They realized that they had said and done some of the things that hurt these parents.

One of the young mothers-to-be, Maria, bravely told us how her little boy died only a few hours after birth. I do not know how or why her little boy died because it seems no one ever told Maria. She didn't get much sympathy and the only way she new how to cope was by becoming pregnant again. She thought that would make the pain go away, but it didn't. The girls in the class hugged her, comforted her and said all the right things. They had listened well and I was proud of what they did for Maria. They decided to have a memorial service for Maria's baby.

There were four girls in the class who had miscarriages. They were slow to mention their miscarriages at first. It seemed they weren't even sure that it was normal for them to mourn for their babies. We listened with horror as they told about some of the cruel things that were said to them. They received little comfort. They were told to get on with their lives. They were told that their baby's death was for the best, that they shouldn't have been pregnant anyway, and that their baby's death was a punishment from God. Few felt comfortable crying in front of family and friends. They had learned to hide their feelings and hold back their tears. By the end of the class we all had stuffy red noses from crying. We were tired. We shared and grew closer during that class. I promised them that I would write a book for young mothers whose babies died, and with their help, I did.

This book was written because of that class, too. At the end of class I casually mentioned that girls who have abortions or make adoption plans for their babies can also grieve deeply. Little did I know what that one statement would do. Three girls came to my office that afternoon. Every one of them had had an abortion. Each one had a story that tore at my heart. They were all mourning for their baby and didn't know it. Their trust in me led me to love them even more than I already did. My love for them and from them has been passed on to you through this book. It was written for teenage women, like you, who never received or had little counseling or comfort after their abortion. It was written for those of you who do not understand your feelings and emotions since your abortion. It was written for those of you who long for peace and forgiveness. It gives you permission to mourn and seek healing.

Tiffany, a young girl, whose face full of tears I will always remember, inspired the title of this book. It is my hope that her pain and her story, as well as those of the other young women, will save you from years of needless suffering. **This book cannot possibly take the place of counseling, post-abortion recovery groups, and the spiritual guidance of the clergy. It is written as a guide to let you know that hope and healing after abortion are possible and that there are many wonderful people out there to encourage and support you.**

"Sorrow makes us all children again."
Ralph Waldo Emerson, American poet

CHAPTER ONE

Tiffany's Story

Tiffany was a troublemaker. You couldn't help but notice her. She was large and loud. She caused fights wherever she went. She questioned everything her teachers said. Her own mother, brothers, and sisters didn't want to be around her. She complained about the teachers, lousy food, being poor, stupid boys, stuck up girls, an unfair world, and the color of the walls. Tiffany was also a top student. She was fair, honest and she defended students that were picked on. She was street wise. Mostly, she was angry and just plain raving mad. Her temper got her in trouble and she was always being sent to the principal's office.

I could never figure out why Tiffany was always so angry, until she came to me after the grief class. She practically knocked me over as she came rushing into my office. "Ohhhh, Connie, have I got something to tell you. You won't believe this, but I've got to tell you."

I had always admired Tiffany for her openness and now I was admiring her big beautiful brown eyes. She looked anxious, scared and angry all at the same time. It seemed she was trying to catch her breath and then she blurted out, "I had four abortions."

I closed my eyes, felt her pain, and in sadness I said, "Tiffany, I'm so sorry."

Before I could ask her if she wanted to tell me about it, she started yelling. "I was fourteen when I had my first abortion. When I got pregnant, I told my mother right away. I did what I was supposed to do. I knew she would be upset, but I never thought she would make me get an abortion. We're Catholic. One morning she woke me up early and told me to get ready. She told me I had an appointment for an abortion. I couldn't believe it. I did what she said, but when I got to the abortion clinic, I cried and begged them not to do the abortion.

1

My mother made such a stink about being poor and not wanting any more babies in the house that they listened to her instead of me. They did the abortion anyway. They didn't even put me to sleep. They said it would cost more. It hurt! It hurt, and they didn't even care! My mother, the doctor, the nurse, nobody cared!" A look of agony spread across her face.

Catching her breath she went on again, "Dalvon was the baby's father. I loved him and I wanted him to be the father of my children. I never told him about the abortion. I just got pregnant again with our second baby. I told my mother as soon as I knew I was pregnant, because I never thought she would make me have another abortion. But she did the same thing and it happened all over again. I begged her not to make me get an abortion. No one listened to me. No one cared. I cried all the way home on the bus and I was cramping. Dalvon and I broke up after that. I couldn't tell him about the abortions. I felt bad because his babies were dead and he never even knew he was a father."

Calmer then, but stone faced she said, "After that I didn't care what happened to me. I partied. I drank. I did crack. I had sex with anyone who asked and I got pregnant again. I waited until I was five months pregnant before I told my mother. She brought me to the doctor and he said it wasn't too late to have an abortion. Why did they keep doing this to me? I had to go to the hospital that time because I was further along. They put something called saline into me. It was awful. I could feel the baby kicking and fighting. Then the baby stopped kicking and I knew it was dead. I started having labor pains the next day. The pains were awful. I didn't want my mother in the room with me because I thought she was evil. We fought the whole time. I told her to go home. I wanted to have my baby alone. A part of me kept hoping that the baby would be alive and then they'd have to save it. The pains kept getting longer and stronger. I pushed and then my little boy was born dead. They all left me alone again. No one cared. I cried for about a minute and then I wrapped him in the sheet and put on the light for the nurse. It took fifteen minutes before she even got there."

2

"I'm not even sure who the father of my little girl was. I was six months along before I told my mother about the fourth pregnancy, but it didn't stop her from beating me and pulling my hair. I had another abortion by the same doctor and at the same hospital. I didn't cry. I guess I just got used to it." Then Tiffany stood there in silence, with a look of hatred on her face, her mouth quivering and twisted as if she were daring me to pass judgment on her. She was ready to lash out at me. She was holding back the tears that were welling in her eyes.

"Tiffany," I asked, "have you cried for your babies?"

A puzzled look crossed her face, as if it were the last thing she was expecting me to say. **"No one told me I could cry,"** she said with a surprise in her voice.

Then I realized why Tiffany had told me her story. What she wanted from me was permission to cry like the other girls did in class that day. So I gave it to her. "Tiffany, you can cry all you want. It's normal to cry. You have a right to cry. Your babies are dead and you miss them."

Hearing those words, the tough, city smart Tiffany turned into a hurting broken child. She held out her arms to me and sobbed, "Hold me. Hold me." I hugged her, rocked her and smoothed her hair. Together we wept.

I knew I had to do something special for Tiffany. She was seven months pregnant and this time she insisted on having the baby and raising it herself. I didn't know much about post-abortion counseling then. What I did know was that if I didn't do something soon it would affect her and her baby for the rest of their lives.

That night I stopped by the library. I took home every book about abortion that the library carried. I read pro-choice books, pro-life books, and the stories of women of all ages who have suffered from abortion. I sent for studies from professional journals and for information from organizations. I spoke with women who had abortions and women who led post-abortion support groups. This book will tell you what I learned and what I shared with Tiffany.

3

"He truly sorrows who sorrows unseen."
Marcus Valarius Martialis, 86 A.D.

"Insults have broken my heart, and I am in despair.
I had hoped for sympathy, but there was none;
for comfort, but I found none."
Psalms 69:20

CHAPTER TWO

A Secret Sorrow

When someone dies, a wake and funeral are held in memory of the one you love. Friends and family come to show respect and give comfort. Flowers, cards, and letters are sent. Prayers are said. Neighbors bring meals. You are allowed to cry in public and people don't mind if you talk about your loved one. People let you mourn.

With abortion, there isn't any wake or funeral. You really don't know where your baby is or what they did with it. If friends and family knew about the abortion, they probably went with you because they knew you were scared. Maybe they tried to comfort you by saying, "Soon, it will all be over," meaning the surgery would soon be over. No one talked about the fact that your baby's life would soon be over. No one prayed for your baby. There weren't any flowers or sympathy cards. Those close to you took care of you long enough to make sure you didn't get sick afterwards. Someone may have made you soup for a day or two because you were "sick." They probably didn't realize that you appreciated the soup because you were too sad to make a meal for yourself. Perhaps they even let you cry for a day or even a week. Then you were told to "be happy," after all now you wouldn't be tied down with a baby. Many times the abortion is never talked about again. You are expected to keep it a secret or pretend it never happened.

There is a special term used to describe this secret sorrow. It is called "disenfranchised grief"[1]. This is a grief that cannot be shown in public, is not allowed by family and friends or is not recognized by others. In abortion, no one mourns because no one has admitted that your baby's life has ended. You should also know that it is harder to mourn when there isn't any body.

If you made your decision to abort by yourself, you and those at the abortion clinic are the only people who know about your abortion. Teens who make their decision alone usually do so because of fear. You may have been afraid of what your boyfriend, parents, or friends would say. Maybe you were afraid of losing their love, disappointing them or hurting them. Perhaps you were worried about raising a child yourself.

If you had dreams for college, you might have thought they would have to end with the baby's birth. Deep shame and guilt might have caused you to make your decision for abortion. You did not want anyone to know you were pregnant. The problem is that if you are the only one that knows about your abortion, you must cry in secret.

"After an abortion many girls go to their room and cry in secret."

You must not show your emotions. You must cover them up and hide them. This takes a lot of energy, so you put it out of your mind. You may have gone back to school or work as if nothing had happened. You did not and are not letting yourself mourn for your baby. You may even be thinking that you do not have a right to grieve because you chose to have the abortion. Maybe, by now, you have hidden your feelings so deeply that you think you do not need to grieve. Maybe you think you are already over the abortion.

Even if you told your family or friends, you will still have to hide your sorrow. One mental health caregiver says that, "Abortion is one of those unspeakable losses that people would rather forget."[2] Young people have an even more difficult time getting sympathy after an abortion loss because:

1. Parents don't want to talk about it. They are angry because you have created a problem for them. It would be too painful for them to think of the fetus as their

grandchild or to admit that they influenced you or forced you to end the life of your own child. It is easier to pretend that "it wasn't really a baby yet" or that the baby never lived in you. They reason that you are young and will have other children.

2. Brothers and sisters may be angry with you, too. Younger brothers and sisters may think of you as having killed your baby. Older brothers and sisters may think of you as being foolish for not using birth control. They may all be angry with you because you have put your family into a crisis. Parents may be fighting more. Brothers and sisters may start acting out to get attention.

3. If your friends approved of the abortion, they probably didn't understand that you were losing your baby. If your friends did not approve of the abortion, they understood that a baby's life was being lost. What they didn't realize was how hard it was to make the decision to abort your baby.

4. Society does not recognize loss after abortion. Some teens who have cried in the abortion clinic have been asked by their own doctor or nurse, "What are you crying for, isn't this what you wanted?" Another teen said she was told by her nurse, "You should be thanking us instead of crying. We've taken care of your problem for you. Now you don't have a care in the world." People will allow you to rest for a day, but they don't want to hear about how the abortion was done or if it hurt. You are expected to go right back to work or school. Your doctor might have given you a gym excuse for a week, but it was probably for stomach upset or cramps. You must pretend it didn't happen. No one wants to hear the truth.

7

In the end, you are left to deal with your abortion alone. You don't have anyone to turn to. No one understands how you feel. You know you miss your baby, but no one will let you say it. You are sad, but you are afraid to show it. It is natural to grieve for a baby who has lost its life, even a tiny baby who has never been seen or held. Yet, those around you act as if this is strange. No one has bothered to teach you how to grieve. You have probably never heard of the grief process or grief work. If you have been unable to grieve after your abortion because 1) you cannot face it, 2) others won't let you, 3) you didn't think you had a right to, or 4) you don't know how to, then your grief is "unresolved." This means that the grieving isn't over yet. It isn't finished. It hasn't been completely expressed or worked through.

"Every unresolved grief is given expression in some form or another." Helene Deutsch

CHAPTER THREE

When Emotions Overflow

Have you ever seen what happens when someone forgets to turn off the water in the bathroom sink? The sink overflows, the bathroom floods, and the water begins to flow into other rooms of the house. The carpets and furniture in your home become soaked and mildew if they are not dried out fast enough. You respond by working harder and faster. No matter how hard you try, you just can't keep up. You become tired and stressed.

The same thing happens when you try to forget or others try to make you forget that you have had an abortion. Feelings that should have poured out of you were poured into you. Eventually they overflow. These feelings spread into other areas of your life. More problems begin to appear. These problems become worse if they are not faced and dealt with. So you keep yourself as busy as you can so you don't have to think about it. Eventually you just can't do it any more. You become tired and stressed.

There is a name for this stress. It is called Post Abortion Stress. Some people call it Post Abortion Syndrome. It is called PAS for short. PAS occurs when: 1) a woman is unable to talk about her abortion 2) when she is unable to admit or accept the loss of her aborted child and 3) when she does not want to or is afraid to make peace with God. Most women seek help or counseling after an abortion when they begin to feel the stress of guilt. Sometimes they are very aware of their guilt and they will say, "I know I did wrong when I aborted my baby." Others will say, "I've been thinking about my abortion a lot lately. I'm beginning to wonder if I made the right decision." Still others will ask for help by saying, "I just don't feel right. I have this nervous feeling inside me."

Healthy and unhealthy guilt

When you know you have done something wrong, you begin to feel guilty. Guilt is healthy when it leads you to understand that you have hurt someone. Then something inside of you realizes that you need to say "I'm sorry" and ask to be forgiven. Guilt becomes unhealthy when you tell yourself that you are so bad you can never be forgiven. Guilt is the most common symptom of PAS.

Listed below are other symptoms and behaviors that can occur after having an abortion. You may have some or all of them depending on how much the abortion has affected you and how long you have been trying to forget about the abortion. Some of them may frighten you as you read about them, but this is not intended. The reasons for discussing them are:

1. To let you know that others have had these kinds of reactions after their abortion
2. To tell you about the more serious symptoms of PAS so you will be encouraged to prevent them from happening to you
3. To teach you that even if you already have some of the more serious symptoms you can prevent them from becoming long lasting problems

Psychological symptoms

Irritability

Other words for irritability are cranky, crabby, and cross. Little things seem to bother you. People around you wonder why you are angry all the time. They have trouble getting along with you. Remember, Tiffany was even upset about the color of the school walls. It turned out that the same color was used on the walls of the clinic where her first two abortions took place.

Anxiety

This means not being able to relax. Anxiety usually comes from conflict. This conflict can come from the difference of opinions between you and your parents or boyfriend about the abortion. A conflict can also take place within yourself. You may have gone against your own morals and values in order to have the abortion.

Constant thoughts about the baby

Post-abortive teens often have many questions about their unborn baby. You may wonder if your child was a boy or a girl, if your child felt pain during the abortion, and what happened to the baby. You may think about what the baby might have looked like, and what color hair or eyes the baby might have had. This is normal and okay, but if these thoughts keep popping into your head and you can't get rid of them, it may be a danger sign. Sometimes girls become very fond of a child who might have been the same age as their own baby or who might have looked like their child. They want to spend all their time with this child.

Troubled relationships

After abortion, relationships with those close to us begin to change. You may be angry with parents who forced you or talked you into the abortion. Maybe you don't want to be close to them or confide in them any more. You trusted them to protect and support you and your baby, but they didn't. Your parents may be angry because you became pregnant. They do not understand why you are angry with them. They think they did what was best for you and the baby. You may think they did it because they didn't want the neighbors to know. It is not unusual for teenagers to run away after an abortion. Girls eighteen and over often move out of the house or go to college and never come back.

Even if your parents don't know about the abortion, you may be angry with them. You may be asking yourself, "Why did they have to teach me right from wrong? If they weren't so religious, I wouldn't feel so guilty." You know you are keeping something from them. Maybe you have lied about where you were the day of the abortion. Maybe

11

A teenage mother and baby's father rarely stay together after an abortion. you lied about why you weren't feeling so good the week after the abortion. You can't look them in the eye. You begin to avoid them so you won't have to think about the lies or the abortion. You begin to fight with them, just so you won't have to be with them. Your parents are hurt because they don't know what they've done to lose your love and confidence. The lies have come between you. Some teens are angry with their parents because they feel they had to protect them from worry. Others think of their parents as weak and are angry because they think they couldn't have dealt with their pregnancy.

A teenage mother and the baby's father rarely stay together after an abortion. She will begin to realize that he didn't love her if he threatened to leave her. Sometimes the baby's father does not want the mother to have an abortion. He may be so hurt he can't stay with her. At other times they may be angry with themselves and each other. They are feeling guilty because they weren't strong enough or brave enough to protect the life of their baby.

Avoidance

This is avoiding what reminds you of the abortion. Seeing other pregnant women can cause a twinge of pain in an aborted mother's heart. This is especially true if she wanted the baby. Eventually many post-abortive women begin to avoid being with pregnant women or anything that reminds them of the abortion. This can include baby showers, friends and relatives that have babies, toy stores and commercials, the baby aisle at the grocery store or holidays that are for children.

It doesn't stop there. Some girls never drink the type of juice that was served to them after the abortion. Some stop going out with their friends, staying home night after night. Others never go back to the clinic for their checkup. If they have to go someplace that will take them past the abortion clinic or hospital, they'll take another route rather than go down that street. Many girls refuse to see a doctor after their abortion. This is dangerous, especially if you are still sexually active. Sexually transmitted diseases (STD's) that aren't treated lead to infertility. This means you would not be able to have children in the future.

"Seeing other pregnant women can cause a twinge of pain in an aborted mother's heart."

Physical symptoms

Post-abortive teens complain about not sleeping well, sleeping too much or too little. They become restless and can't get comfortable. Nightmares are frightening because they are usually about the baby. Stomach pains and cramping that bring back memories of the abortion are common. Headaches occur often. Some teens that remain sexually active after an abortion talk about sex being painful. Others say they have lost any desire to have sex. Flashbacks which are like living through the abortion again are very common. These flashbacks often bring on a feeling of panic. This is because thoughts of the abortion just pop into your head and they cannot be controlled.

Emotional symptoms

Punishing oneself and self-destructive actions

Some girls feel that they should be punished for having an abortion. They begin doing things to hurt themselves. Other teens realize they are doing things to hurt themselves, but they don't know why. Following is a discussion of some of these harmful acts. They are all signs of extreme depression. If you have any of these symptoms, please get help right away! There are so many people out there who care and are waiting to help you.

1. *Having casual sex with many partners.* When you have sex with many partners, you gamble with your life. You take a chance on getting a

sexually transmitted disease. Many of these diseases cause infertility, which means you won't be able to have any more babies. Having an abortion leaves some girls with such bad and painful memories that they want to become infertile. They reason that if they can't get pregnant, they'll never have to go through another abortion. Some of these diseases such as hepatitis and AIDS can cause death. Dying is seen as a way of ending their pain.

2. *Letting yourself be abused.* Frequently, girls who have had abortions let others punish them. They enter into abusive relationships with men or continue to let their parents abuse them. The abuse can be physical, sexual, or verbal. If she allows herself to be physically abused, she is putting herself in danger of being beaten so brutally that she may eventually lose her own life. Sexual abuse can include being raped by one's partner, or letting yourself be used for perverse acts. Perverse acts are warped or sinful sexual acts and are harmful to one's self esteem. It is an extreme form of self punishment. Verbal abusers keep telling you that you are bad, unwanted, and don't deserve any happiness. They will continually remind you of the abortion by saying things like, "Stay away from the children. I don't want you to hurt them."

3. *Eating disorders.* This means that your eating patterns are unhealthy. Examples of eating disorders are anorexia, bulimia, and obesity. Anorexia means eating so little that you can become malnourished. Many teens have died from anorexia. Often monthly periods will stop if you are anorexic. If your periods stop, you will not release an egg to be fertilized. Some girls want this to happen so they won't become pregnant again. Bulimia starts with extreme hunger and going on a food binge. To relieve the feeling of being stuffed, bulimics make themselves vomit, take laxatives, water pills or give themselves enemas. Any of these practices, when done over a period of time can cause serious heart and liver damage. The vomiting can cause dental decay, sores in the mouth, bleeding from the esophagus (the organ that carries food to your stomach), and gum disease which can cause tooth loss.

Obesity is a condition in which the body becomes very fat and increases your chances of getting high blood pressure and other diseases. Eating disorders usually begin as a response to a strong negative emotion such as depression, self hatred, loneliness, physical or emotional pain, helplessness or hopelessness. Eating disorders are carried out in secret, which causes you to become less social since it must be hidden from friends and family. Appearance becomes less attractive due to extreme thinness or overweight. One reason for wanting to become unattractive is to keep boys and men away from you to avoid pregnancy.

4. *Attempting suicide or thoughts of suicide.* This is a severe form of depression. Many post-abortive teens have suicidal thoughts but they do not really want to die. What they really want is help because they are hurting and missing their baby. If you are having suicidal thoughts, ask for help from a counselor, friend, or clergyman immediately!

5. *Alcohol and drug abuse.* Many post-abortive teens resort to alcohol and drugs to reduce the pain of abortion memories. At first teens will try these substances out of curiosity or for fun. Later they realize that these substances "numbed" them for awhile and want this feeling again and again. Problems add up when they become addicted and are unable to function in school or at work. Using substances will postpone the grief process. The longer the grief process is postponed the more painful it will be.

Worry over future children
The thought of not being able to have other children is a constant worry for some women who have had abortions. Still others are afraid that their other children will be born with a birth defect, become ill or die. They often think these things will happen because, "God is going to punish them."

Wanting to become pregnant again
Sorrow and regret over having an abortion often lead a teen into

thinking that she wants to become pregnant again. When someone has

The anniversary date of an abortion can be a dangerous time. Planning to get through the day by numbing yourself with drugs can lead to addiction.

a baby soon after abortion, the baby is called an "atonement baby." This means that they want to have another baby so they can make up for the abortion. Many times they think that if they become pregnant again and raise the baby that God will forgive them.

Teenage girls often think that having a baby will take away the grief that they are feeling for their aborted baby, but it does not.

Changed relationships with children

Many moms find themselves behaving differently around their older children. Some run themselves ragged trying to do everything for the older child that they couldn't do for their unborn child. Some become overprotective. In some cases mothers begin to act very cool toward their older child. When a woman has an abortion, she has to force herself to become unattached to her unborn child. She does not allow herself to bond with the child. After the abortion this process of becoming unattached can extend to her older or future children. She protects herself from ever knowing the pain and loss of a child again by not bonding with them. Sometimes this leads to child abuse.

Working or studying very hard

If a young girl has had an abortion because she wanted to continue her education she may begin to study hard and constantly. This is so she can prove to herself that she had the abortion for a good reason. If she is saving for college or has already begun a career she will work just as hard for the same reason.

Anniversary syndrome

Around the due date of a baby or a year after an abortion, feelings of sadness, guilt and anxiety can become very intense. Symptoms that you have had before can reoccur at this time, while other symptoms can appear for the first time. Some girls are very aware of these dates and the reason for such strong emotions, yet others are not. When looking back, women remember that they planned to do something to help them forget the importance of the date such as partying, drinking, or doing drugs.

When Does Post Abortion Syndrome Begin?

Post Abortion Syndrome can begin right after abortion or may not be recognized until fifty years later. Those who work with post-abortive women have begun to ask themselves why there is such a difference in years in recognizing symptoms. One reason comes from the medical and mental health community itself. For years experts have argued over whether or not there are any serious effects after abortion. Thirty years ago, if a woman was affected by an abortion, she really didn't have anywhere to turn. Since abortion was illegal, women sought help for emotional pain and depression, but were careful not to mention the abortion. Counselors were not able to tie the two together.

Secondly, those who began treating post-abortive women for emotional problems after abortion became legal, noticed similar symptoms among post-abortive women, but they didn't have a name for it.

Lately, health workers and counselors have noticed that more and more teens and college students want to talk to them about their abortion. They are unsure of how they should be feeling after an abortion. One reason for this is the invention of ultrasound technography. An ultrasound helps a doctor to know how long a mother has been carrying her baby. A picture of the baby is taken. Young women often go with their friends or relatives when an ultrasound is being done. They can see the baby's heart beating and watch the baby swimming in its mother. Another reason is that students are shown movies and photos of unborn babies in school, so more girls are aware of how a baby grows. As a result, teens are beginning to have symptoms of PAS earlier and are asking for help.

CHAPTER FOUR

What You Should Know About Teenagers and Abortion

About 1,000,000 girls between the ages of eleven and nineteen become pregnant every year. About 330,000 of these girls end their pregnancies with abortion.[3] You are not alone. More than likely you probably know several girls who have had abortions. You may not know exactly who they are because they are trying to keep their abortion a secret.

Studies have been done to find out how abortion affects teenagers. This is what we learned from them.

1. Abortion can be more stressful for a teenager than for an adult.[4-5]
2. Adolescents are more likely to develop psychological problems after an abortion.[6-8]
3. Teenagers who report "being particularly fond of children" do not do as well psychologically after an abortion.[9]
4. Teenagers who abort are more likely to be admitted to mental health hospitals than teens in general.[10]
5. Girls under eighteen experience more guilt and are more uncertain if abortion was the right choice for them.[11]
6. Adolescents who do not mourn after an abortion have a greater risk of getting pregnant again soon after the abortion.[12]
7. One study found that when adolescent girls were asked if they would have an abortion again, 66% said "no".[13]
8. Teenage mothers who have had abortions are twice as likely to use alcohol, marijuana, or cocaine.[14]
9. Teenagers have more nightmares about the abortion.[15]

19

10. Teens are more likely to attempt suicide after an abortion.[16,17]

11. Adolescents have a higher rate of second trimester abortions (abortions done during the fourth, fifth or sixth month of pregnancy). This is a concern because abortions done in the second trimester are a greater mental and physical health risk.[18]

"Young men, whose girlfriends or wives have had an abortion against their wishes, struggle more with their feelings."

12.   Middle adolescents, aged 15-17, are most likely to have a repeat pregnancy and suffer more from depression. The abortion decision is hardest for the late adolescent, aged 18-21. More likely, she loves the father of her baby and their relationship is the most likely to continue after the abortion.[19]

Besides being young, there may be other reasons why coping with abortion may be difficult for you.[20] This list includes:

- having mixed feelings about the pregnancy and the baby
- a strong religious background
- going against your own moral beliefs
- being or feeling pressured to have the abortion
- having an abortion late in pregnancy
- wanting to raise the baby but unable to find a way to do so
- it was your first pregnancy
- you have a strong love for your baby
- you had little or no support from family or the baby's father
- you love your baby's father
- the relationship with your baby's father has ended
- you may have other problems such as being raped or abused, the death of a relative or close friend, neglectful and substance abusing parents

"I wasn't in the room: I wasn't even in the clinic that day. But in my mind, I've been there a million times since. I've been there watching, breaking, wanting to rescue you. In my mind I need to be a hero not a killer, the man who didn't flee. But I am not. I am the man I fear to see."[21]

CHAPTER FIVE

How Abortion Affects Young Fathers

A special effort has been made to include young dads in this book because they are often forgotten. There is little help for the young mother of an aborted baby and even less support for a young father. If you are a teen yourself or a little older, it will help you to read this chapter and go through the grief and healing process.

Abortion Attitudes of Young Men

Whether or not it is a long lasting or a casual relationship, most young men want to be included in making an abortion decision. Young men have also expressed a need for emotional support during this difficult time. When these needs aren't recognized he feels confused and ignored.[22] Two groups of young men seem to struggle more after an abortion. The first group are those whose girlfriends or wives had an abortion against their wishes. The second group of men are those who were taught that "abortion is a woman's issue" and wanted to support the decision of their partner. Because they were trying to be supportive, they denied their own feelings of wanting to prevent the abortion and put up a "strong front." These men tell about feelings of anxiety, helplessness, guilt, self-blame, and regret.[23] Some young men have told that they have felt rage and total despair as well as expressing fear that their partners would leave them.[24] Men whose teenage girlfriends have had an abortion have more stress as adults than men who became young and teen fathers.[25]

The Effects of Abortion on Young Men

Many young men are coming forward to say that abortion has deeply affected them and you may feel the same way. Perhaps you are wondering why you are troubled by the abortion. A counselor who works with men whose babies have been aborted says that one of the reasons is because you know that deep down inside you are responsible for the abortion decision, too. That decision will affect the rest of your life.[26] Another reason is that you have gone against your own fatherly instincts, which are to protect and provide for your children.

Abortion is the loss of a child. It is normal to feel pain after a loss and abnormal not to express it, but our culture puts up roadblocks that stand in the way of a young man who is having pain after an abortion. In short, you don't have much of a support system. Like your partner, you may have had to keep it a secret from your parents. If your parents know, they are probably relieved that you and they do not have to be responsible for supporting the child. If you tried to tell your partner about your sorrow, she may have come back with "You didn't have to go through the pregnancy," or "You didn't have to have the abortion." Friends have probably said, "You got away easy." No one understands that you have lost your child. Although you did not have to go through the physical trauma of having an abortion, you cannot escape the emotional hurt.

Gary Bell, President of Dads for Life, expressed it in this way:

"The death of your children is very difficult to cope with in any case, but with abortion it is a death that goes unrecognized by society. There's no funeral, no gathering of friends and family, no choice to grieve openly, no chance to say good bye. I can remember just wanting someone to know, wanting someone, anybody, to acknowledge my loss, wanting someone to tell me it was okay to grieve. "[27]

What can you do when you have to keep the abortion a secret, you can't find anyone who is willing to let you show your grief, or you refuse to grieve? It leaves you with poor choices that can only make the pain go away for a little while. You can

"Alcohol will only take away the pain for a little while."

pressure your partner to become pregnant again to replace the unborn child. This usually backfires because the same reasons for having the first abortion are still present during the second pregnancy. A repeat abortion may occur. If the second child is born, both you and the mother will go through depression once you realize that no child can replace another child.

The second thing you can do is stuff and bury your feelings. You simply forget about the abortion. This is called repression, but repression leads you to express your feelings in a harmful way. You may feel rage for a very slight reason and take it out on the wrong person in the wrong way. You may become violent or abusive toward women. Before abortion became legal, many people thought that abortion would reduce the number of unwanted children in the world. They reasoned that if there were fewer unwanted children there would be less child abuse. Instead, woman and child abuse has multiplied fourteen times since abortion became legal.[28]

Repression can also lead to self destruction by "living life in the fast lane." Examples are drinking and driving, putting yourself in dangerous places such as burglary attempts or drug deals, taking dares, and engaging in risky activities such as sky diving, drag racing, and mountain climbing.

Other things you may have tried to get rid of the pain are drugs and alcohol. It starts out by saying to yourself, "I want to have a good time, just for tonight." It felt good and you may have blacked out. So you want to do it again. Pretty soon it takes more drugs and more alcohol to make you feel that good again. Then you have a full blown addiction and out of control problems.

A male expert who works with fathers of aborted babies says that repression can lead to a "fear lifestyle." Men may be "afraid that they cannot handle it in the future...they protect themselves so it doesn't happen again...they will not have relationships, they will not trust women...they will not feel comfortable around pregnant women or crying children. . . These things poke at you."[29]

Relationships and Abortion

Seventy percent of all couples break up after an abortion. In more serious relationships, about twenty-five percent of couples break up.[30]

"Abortion has never been known to solve any relationship problems. The only time couples report feeling closer after an abortion is when they have mutually shared feelings of grief and regret about having aborted their child. In short, the relief of being freed from an unplanned pregnancy never binds a couple closer together, but honestly shared remorse can."[31]

One of the reasons for breakups after abortion is because it isn't talked about. Couples are afraid their partner will become upset or that they will end up fighting. In the mean time, both of you are probably feeling sad and guilty. If you bury these feelings together it can lead to depression, substance abuse, sexual dysfunction, demanding behavior, and violence. The abortion must be talked about so you can bring out the emotions surrounding it. Hiding these emotions from one another will keep you apart. Feelings and emotions are hard to show, especially for men. Most men were taught to hide their tears and feelings of love, but that it was okay to express anger. As a result, anger is used to cover up the real feelings that you have.

The abortion is a big part of your relationship now. It is about the death of your child. If you cannot talk about something as important as your child, you will not be able to talk about other things that are important to you. You and your partner will lose your feelings of love for each other because you have to spend so much energy protecting each other from pain and suffering. Bringing the abortion out in the open will not be easy, but letting it come between you by not talking about it will be harder and probably end the relationship. Here are some ground rules that you can follow when discussing the abortion:

1. Accept each other's feelings. Never say to your partner, "You have no right to feel that way." Feelings are neither right nor wrong. They just are.
2. Use this communication model. "When you... I felt or I feel....because". Some examples are:

"When you were having the abortion, I felt powerless because I couldn't stop you from doing it."
"When you said you were having an abortion, I felt like a baby myself and I wanted to cry because I knew how much you really wanted the baby and I couldn't figure out a way to take care of you and the baby."
"When I insisted that you have an abortion, I was scared because I didn't think I would be a good father. Now I feel like I can never forgive myself because I hurt you and my baby."

This model will help you to avoid blaming each other and be honest and open about your feelings.

3. Try to feel your partner's pain and hurt. Hug and comfort each other.
4. Invite God into your relationship. Pray together for both of you to heal. Ask God to bring you closer together in His sight. Seek forgiveness from each other, your baby, yourself and from God.

> *"He forgives all my sins and heals all my diseases.*
> *He keeps me from the grave*
> *and blesses me with love and mercy.*
> *He fills my life with good things,*
> *so that I stay young and strong like an eagle.*
> **Psalm 103:3-5**

If You and Your Baby's Mother Are No Longer Together

If you have lost your baby and your partner, you have twice the heartache. Just the same, it remains important that you grieve for your baby and the end of your love for one another. Casual relationships do

"Avoid blaming each other. Try to feel your partner's pain and hurts. Hug and comfort each other."

not make it any less easy to grieve for your aborted baby. The trauma of abortion will always be there, even though it might not have been hard for you to walk away from your baby's mother.

You are a post-abortive father and always will be. Grief, healing, forgiveness, and hope are necessary in order for you to love again. When you fall in love again, tell your loved one about the abortion. Keeping the abortion a secret, or keeping any secrets will prevent you from showing trust in your partner. Trust is a key issue in any relationship and a lack of trust blocks closeness. If you do not tell your partner everything about you, you will not allow her to love all that you are and that includes your faults, mistakes and sins. Forgive yourself, love yourself, and let yourself love fully.

CHAPTER SIX

How Teenagers Deal with Abortion

Most teenagers don't have any real counseling before or after an abortion. Young girls have reported that before the abortion they were shown pictures of a "baby" but that it looked like a piece of meat. Other young women have said that they were put in a room and all the women having abortions on that day were told how the abortion would be done. Young men seem to have more questions about the abortion because they are worried about their baby's mother, but say they are just left alone in the waiting room to deal with it. After their abortion, young women say they were taught how to take care of themselves for the next few days. Some say they were given a lecture about birth control and then given free birth control pills. Others have been told they would be depressed for a few days because of a change in hormones but then it would go away.

The most common reaction for teenagers after abortion is relief. This may be because they feared the surgery itself and now it is over. They are relieved of having to make any more hard decisions under pressure. They no longer have to worry about telling their parents or supporting a baby. Sadly, this feeling of relief only lasts for a short while. Many problems that teenagers face before the abortion are still there after the abortion. Parents may still be abusive, grades are still poor, and a boyfriend, or spouse still wants to end the relationship. Instead of fixing the problem through pregnancy, the pregnancy became another problem. It is an experience of death and the loss must be faced.

Many care givers in abortion clinics deny that there are any problems after an abortion. As a result, women are not told about the kinds of emotional or health problems that can occur. When teenagers recognize problems after abortion, they begin to wonder what is wrong with them. Since they have been told that there aren't any problems or that there are few problems after abortion, they keep it to themselves. They try to ignore their feelings about the abortion or they just try to forget about it. These are some of the replies that a group of teenagers gave when they were asked how they handled their feelings after abortion.

Cassandra, a 17 year old National Honor Society student wrote, "I told myself to forget about it. I felt I had to get on with my life. So I worked long hours at work, filling in for others when they needed me and always working overtime. I was trying to save money for college. I became active in student council and was a cheerleader. I got good grades and stayed on the honor roll. I also sang in the church choir. I guess I did everything I could to stop myself from thinking about my baby."

Tawanda answered the question in this way. "I stayed in the weekend after my abortion. I just cried and cried and cried. The next weekend I decided I was tired of crying and I wanted to go out and have a good time. My friends took me to a party to help me to forget about it. They bought me a six pack as a gift and then pulled out the bud (marijuana). It made me feel "numb" and then "high". I liked feeling this way on weekends. It was a relief. This went on for about a year. After that the bud and beer didn't seem to help any more. I knew the next step would be crack or ice or heroin. I didn't want to do this, but I didn't know how to stop the pain either. Finally, I knew I had to ask someone for help. Jesus must have been watching over me 'cause the youth minister in our church told me exactly where to go for post-abortion counseling. The way I saw it, I had two choices. I could go on having "fun" or I could get rid of this bad feeling I had about myself."

Jamie said, "I must have been dreaming about my baby during the abortion. I woke up crying and screaming 'I want my baby back.' The nurses told me to be quiet and gave me a shot to calm me down so I wouldn't upset the other patients. I was told I could have another baby later. So that's what I did. Two months after my abortion I got pregnant again. I told everyone that this time I was keeping my baby.

After a while everyone was happy about it. When the doctor put the baby on my stomach after it was born I was so happy, but then I thought to myself, 'Where is my other baby?'."

Some girls cope with their abortion by using rationalization. This means that they convince themselves that having an abortion was the only thing that made sense at the time. "My parents said that if I had the baby they would kick me out of the house. How could I have a baby if I didn't have any place to live?" In most states, if you were under eighteen, your parents couldn't have kicked you out of the house. They would have been reported to the Department of Children and Family Services. Social service agencies and crisis pregnancy centers also have lists of maternity and private homes where you can stay if you find yourself homeless or living in a difficult situation.

Marilyn recalls "I knew about places where pregnant girls could go, but fighting with my parents left me weak. I didn't have the strength or the know-how to find one."

Donetta and Marvin had been dating for two years. They both wanted to keep the baby, but they reasoned, "We wanted to be mature. We wanted to take care of things ourselves. We were only sixteen, and we wanted to finish school. There were things we wanted to do before we had a baby. We didn't have the money to take care of the baby anyway. It was the best thing to do for all of us."

Why can't I go on this way? I'm doing just fine.

You can go on this way. No one is going to force you to change your thoughts or actions. You may be doing just fine for now, but it would be a lie to say that you will always feel okay about the abortion. By working through your grief now, instead of later, you can prevent yourself from having the many long term problems of post-abortion syndrome. You won't waste years crying and suffering. Hope and healing are just around the corner if you are willing to grieve, forgive and make peace with God.

CHAPTER SEVEN

Getting Ready to Grieve

Grief is an emotion and response that you feel after losing someone or something that was important to you. While you are grieving for your baby, you may discover other losses that you were never given the chance to grieve for properly. These losses can include the death of a parent, other close relative, a friend or a pet. Adopted teens feel the loss of their birth parents, but society does not view this as a loss since they have been loved by their adoptive family. This is another example of "disenfranchised grief". You may feel a loss of love if you have been physically, sexually, or verbally abused.

Teens who have been neglected also feel a loss of love. Your mother or father may have walked out when you were little. Perhaps, you seldom or never see them. Parents that are alcohol or drug addicted neglect their children because they are unable to think about anything but getting their next drink or their next hit. Other parents neglect their children by being workaholics. They have put their jobs before their children.

If your family moves around a lot, as military families do, you have had to say good-bye to a lot of friends. Maybe you've only had to move once, but it was several hours away from where you lived. Perhaps your best friend has moved away. Saying good-bye to friends is especially hard on teenagers.

If your parents have divorced, you must also grieve for the family that you once were or might have been. You probably miss the parent that has moved out of the house. The same thing can be said for a brother or sister that has moved in with your other parent. Getting divorced or the end of a relationship also has to be mourned.

Sadly, death and loss are a part of everyday life. What you learn about the art and skills of grieving from this book can be used any time.

Grief work

Grief work means going through the tasks that are needed to come through grief in a healthy way. It is hard and painful work, but you will grow and learn through your sorrow. There are steps that you can take to prepare yourself to grieve.

1. Know that grieving takes time. There isn't a time limit on grief. Everyone grieves in their own way and in their own time. Many believe that grief is timeless and a lifelong process.

2. Get support. Although you may think this book is all you need, support from someone that counsels post-abortive women and men will be a great help to you. A good post-abortion counselor is someone who is familiar with and knows about PAS. Your counselor will not judge or condemn you. A good counselor will give you love and compassion. At the same, your counselor will help you to accept the responsibility of your abortion.

    The easiest way to find a qualified counselor is to call one of the crisis pregnancy organizations listed in the "Where To Get Help" section at the back of the book. They can put you in touch with over 4,000 local crisis pregnancy centers in the United States and Canada. Many of the women who work in crisis pregnancy centers have had abortions themselves. They have had training in post-abortion counseling and know what you are going through. Some of the centers also provide services for young husbands and boyfriends who have a difficult time following abortion. Many of these centers also keep a list of psychologists, psychiatrists, and clergy that are willing to help and are familiar with PAS. Work with a psychological and spiritual counselor. Complete healing can only take place if both these areas of your life are cared for.

3. Try to find a support group. This may be a problem for you. Many crisis pregnancy centers have started support groups for post-

abortive women, but these support groups are usually attended by adults. Young people say they feel uncomfortable in them. In the past, childbirth education classes and grief support groups for parents were mostly attended by adults, too. In recent years, however, childbirth education classes and grief support groups for teenagers have sprung up all over. This is because care givers learned

"A good counselor will give you love and compassion."

that teenagers need and do better in groups that are for teens only. Right now there are few "teen only" post-abortion support groups. If you are interested in joining a "teen only" post-abortion support group, let your local crisis pregnancy center know. Groups will form if you let them know that this is something young women need. In the meantime, joining a post-abortion support group for women of all ages might be very helpful to you. You can benefit from their love, sharing, and wisdom.

There are even fewer post-abortion groups for men, but more and more are being started. It is worth calling your local crisis pregnancy center to see if they have one. A few organizations have recently formed for the sole purpose of supporting the post-abortive male.

4. If you cannot find a counselor or support group, contact one of the organizations listed in the Where to Get Help section that offer post-abortion workbooks and Bible studies. These studies and workbooks will aid you in answering many of your own questions and put you in touch with your feelings.

5. Keep a diary or journal. Writing is a good way to clear up your thoughts and feelings about your abortion. As time goes on, you will see that you are making progress. You will learn some things about yourself that will lead you in a new direction. This journal will also be a good place to let out your anger. You can write a

letter to your parents, boyfriend or husband, or doctor. You can write to God about your anger, worries and fears and start a new and loving relationship with Him. Writing about or to your baby will put you in touch with the loving feelings you have for your baby.

6. Buy a sketchpad, or recording tape. Some people can express themselves better by drawing, painting, sketching, and writing or recording music and poetry.

"Those who weep recover more quickly than those who smile. "
Jean Giraudous, 1882-1944, French dramatist and diplomat

CHAPTER EIGHT

The Grief Process

As you grieve, you will pass through certain phases. Each phase has certain feelings, acts, thoughts and tasks that go along with it. These phases do not always occur in order. You may go back and forth between phases or go through several phases at the same time. Your emotions will go up and down like a roller coaster. This is normal. These phases are discussed here so you will know what to expect.

Denial

Having an abortion, seeing a friend murdered, or being raped are examples of frightful events. The deep pain that comes with these traumatic happenings is just too painful to face all at once. Your mind will protect itself from falling to pieces. One way to do this is to deny that anything has happened. Denial will help you for the moment. It can get you past the crisis, but it shouldn't last for a long time. The longer you stay in denial the harder it will be for you to get past it.

The heartache of aborting a baby is so intense that some women never want to talk or think about it again. Deep shame and guilt can also keep you in denial. Some women purposely give the wrong phone number at the abortion clinic so they cannot be contacted again. Others, when asked if they have ever had an abortion, will say "no", even if asked by their doctor. If you are Rh negative, this can be harmful to your next baby. You need to receive a special medicine before you become pregnant again. Women who are in denial say things such as these:

"I don't believe that babies have souls before they are born, so I didn't really end a life."

35

"The doctor told me it was just two periods and some water. It wasn't a baby yet."

"I didn't have an abortion. I had a wad of tissue removed that could have become a baby."

"I was raped, I couldn't think of it as a baby. It was a monster that ruined my life."

"They said what I was carrying wasn't a baby. It had so many birth defects, the best it could be was a vegetable."

Some young women deny the selfishness of those that wanted them to have the abortion.

"My boyfriend told me, 'Get rid of the kid or I'm gone.' If we were married he wouldn't have said that. He loves me."

"My mother said that if I had the baby she wouldn't help me. She only said that because she really cares about me and wanted me to have a college education."

You may recognize these actions or thoughts of denial in yourself. You should know that for now it may make things seem less painful, but denial can only cover your grief for so long.

Asking yourself these questions will help you become aware of your own denial.

1. Have I ever insisted that it wasn't really a baby that I aborted?
2. Do I try not to think about the abortion?
3. Do I try not to think about the baby?
4. Do I tell myself that I have no baby to grieve for?
5. Do I avoid thinking of myself as a mother?
6. Do I deny that I loved my baby?
7. Do I deny that my baby was a human being?
8. Do I keep telling myself, "The abortion was no big deal?"
9. Do I blame others for the abortion to avoid feeling guilty?

Most young women are relieved after the abortion is over with, but a few hours, days, or months later you may find yourself thinking, "I can't believe I did it." Some of the feelings that go along with denial are shock, emotional numbness, and disbelief. Gabriella told her counselor, "I cried so hard after the abortion. I told myself I couldn't keep crying or everyone would know. The problem is I didn't just stop crying, I stopped laughing, too. I don't think I have any feelings left."

You can keep yourself in denial by avoiding anything that reminds you of the abortion. Young people often stay in denial because they can't face the part that they played in having the abortion. Some are afraid that God will condemn them if they admit their guilt. Just the opposite is true. God is all forgiving.

There are a few tasks to work through in order to get past denial. One is to recognize your losses. Recognizing your losses is heart breaking. It will be very painful, but by naming what you have lost, you can begin to work on what needs to be grieved. The following questions will help you to figure out what you have lost. You can write about them in your journal. Take your time. Grieving cannot be rushed. Don't try to answer the questions all at once. Take several days, weeks or even months to think about your losses and how they have changed you. If you find yourself weeping, don't hold back the tears. Tears are part of the healing process.

- Do you feel like you have lost a part of yourself? Have you lost your baby to abortion? Do you know if it was a boy or a girl?

- Do you understand that you can never bring your baby back? Do you know you have lost the chance to hold the baby you aborted?

- Have you lost your innocence? Have you lost your childhood?

- Have you lost respect for yourself? Have you lost self-esteem? Have you lost sight of your goals for the future?

- Have you lost your health? Have you had any health problems because of your abortion?

- Have you had any losses due to drug abuse, drinking, or eating disorders since your abortion?

- Have you lost good relationships and entered into abusive relationships?

- Have you lost the ability to say no to anyone that asks you to have sex with them?

- Have you lost interest in taking care of yourself? Do you care about how you look? Do you take risks that would put your life in danger? Do you try to hurt yourself?

- Have you lost your desire to have other children?

- Have you lost your hope for marriage to your partner?

- Did your relationship with your parents change when you became pregnant? How has it changed? Have you lost their trust? Have you lost their respect? Have you lost their love?

- If your parents talked you into or forced you to have an abortion, have you lost respect for them? Have you lost your trust in them? Have you lost the ability to love them? Do you love them less?

- If you never told your parents about the pregnancy or abortion, are you still being honest with them? Are you still able to look them in the eye? Do you feel as close to them as you did before the abortion?

- Did your relationship with your baby's father change? Did he leave you after the pregnancy? Was he angry because you had the abortion? Did you fight more? Has he abused you in any way since the abortion? Do you still have respect for each other? Are you further apart or closer emotionally? Have you lost your ability to trust him or other men?

"Sometimes you cry so hard you begin to feel numb and you think you don't have any feelings left."

- If you have an older child, do you find yourself losing your temper with this child more often? Are you treating your child differently? Are you overprotective? Are you less attached to this child? Are you hurting or not taking good care of your child?

- Have you lost any friendships? Have your friendships changed?

- Have you lost your faith? Have you lost sight of God's presence in your life? Do you think God still loves you? Are you afraid of God? Have you lost God's peace?

- Have you lost others that you loved through death, divorce, a move, alcoholism, or addiction? Have you ever been physically, sexually, or verbally abused?

Thinking about your losses will bring out feelings of sadness and longing for what you have lost, but this is not enough. It is important to get in touch with all of your feelings. Some girls find that it helps to hold a doll or teddy bear and pretend that they are talking to their baby.

Get support from a crisis pregnancy center counselor, health care worker, or clergyperson who is familiar with the treatment of post-abortion counseling. They will gently take you through the trauma of the abortion by helping you to remember the circumstances that led up to the abortion. They will ask you to remember where the abortion took place. You will be asked to use all your senses in describing the abortion. Your counselor will listen to what you felt, heard, said, and saw. Your anger and sorrow will be deeply felt, but a postabortion counselor will be able to get you through this. This is the toughest task of grieving after an abortion.

You may find yourself sobbing or raging for hours, but this cannot hurt you. It is the denial of your feelings that can hurt you. God in His wisdom knows this.

> *"Listen to the Lord, you women,*
> *and pay attention to his words.*
> *Teach your daughters how to mourn,*
> *and your friends how to sing a funeral song."*
> *Jeremiah 9:30*

Another thing that you can do to pass through denial is to name your baby. Naming your baby will comfort you. It gives you the opportunity to acknowledge your baby as a person. It will allow you to express your tender feelings of love for your baby. It will give your baby the respect and dignity that a human being deserves.

One concern that mothers have is how to name the baby if they do not know if it was a boy or a girl. Many mothers say they have a strong feeling of knowing if it was a boy or a girl and will then name their baby. Others say they have seen their baby in a dream. Still others choose to give their baby a name that can be used for a boy or a girl. You can name your baby privately or in a special memorial service held with your counselor or clergyperson. They will help you to pick out special Bible verses, prayers, or songs that you would like to have included in the service.

Another concern of aborted mothers is that they do not have a grave or marker for the baby. There are memorial grounds and buildings for aborted babies that allow you to purchase a plaque or a marker with your baby's name on it. This is reassuring to many mothers since they know their babies will not be forgotten. The "Where To Get Help" section at the back of the book can tell you how to get in touch with them.

Anger

Feeling angry is neither good nor bad. It is a feeling. Teenagers seem to have more anger after an abortion because so many are forced, threatened, or talked into having an abortion. Remember how the littlest thing could make Tiffany angry? It is important for young women to know that:

"...no abortion decision is ever made in a vacuum. It is born of influences, pressures, fears, agendas, plans and many other factors. Most women seem to feel it was the only option, the only choice possible. Friends and family, who could and should have provided the support to prove otherwise, failed to do so... Her right to choose was never a choice at all."[32]

Knowing this, you can understand why you may be feeling angry with the baby's father, family, friends, health care worker, or anyone else who may have influenced you.

Being angry with those that did the abortion. Teenage women are more likely to say they weren't satisfied with the kind of care they received at the abortion clinic. Many girls felt that they were told a lie.

"They never said the word baby. They called my baby an embryo and showed me a picture of something that was red and spongy looking. They made me believe it wasn't real.: About six months after my abortion I saw a movie about how a baby grows inside the mother. It said the heart starts beating about three weeks and that it has brain waves at seven weeks. I learned that embryo means "little one" and then I saw an embryo that was seven weeks. It didn't look nothin' like what they showed me. You could see the head and eyes and arms and legs. After awhile I couldn't look any more. I got sick and had to run to the bathroom. That was what my baby looked like. They didn't show me the right picture."

Other words that have been used instead of baby to describe an abortion are "uterine contents", "tissue", "fetal matter", "birth matter", "parasite", "products of conception", "two periods and some water", "liquid" and "a blob". What you should have been told is that an abortion ends the life of an unborn baby, a human being in its early stages.

You will probably feel a lot of anger towards your baby's father. It doesn't matter if he was supportive or not. He may have denied that he was the father of the baby. Maybe he just ran away and left you. Maybe he didn't want you to have the abortion but couldn't or wouldn't help support the baby. He may have said he'd leave you if you didn't have the abortion and then broke up with you anyway. Some girls say they have been beaten when their boyfriends or husbands found out they were pregnant. Even if he said he would support you in your choice you may still be angry. As one girl put it, "I couldn't see how we could take care of a baby. There wasn't any

"Handle your anger by writing about it in your journal or in a letter."

other way to solve the problem. He wanted me to have the baby, but also said that it was my choice. If he wanted me to have the baby so bad, why didn't he run in and say, 'Stop! We'll find a way to keep the baby.'?"

You may be angry with your parents. Parents often refuse to help take care of a baby or threaten to kick you out of the house. Sometimes they just want you to have an abortion because they are afraid of what friends, family, and neighbors will say. Some honestly believe that having a baby will ruin your life and your chances for an education. You may question your parents' love for you if they forced you to have an abortion. It may seem that they didn't care about your feelings or protecting you and your baby.

Perhaps your parents were very helpful and supportive and you wonder why you may be angry with them. Many girls who insisted on having an abortion become angry when their parents didn't try to stop them. Other parents may be so neglectful or addicted that they didn't know or care that you were pregnant or had an abortion.

Being angry with God is scary. The thought of expressing anger to the creator is scary because you may be afraid that He will become angry with you. You may think He will punish you by allowing more trouble to come into your life. God is understanding and the best way to handle your anger toward God is to tell Him honestly as if you were praying. You may be angry with God because He let you become pregnant. Maybe you're angry with Him because He didn't make it possible for you to keep your baby. Whatever you do, tell your Father in heaven how you feel. He's the best Father you can have. He is loving, caring, and forgiving and soon you will feel His comfort.

> *"His anger lasts only a moment,*
> *His goodness for a lifetime.*
> *Tears may flow in the night,*
> *but joy comes in the morning."*
> **Psalm 30:5**

You should know that feeling angry towards the aborted baby is common. If you have angry feelings toward your baby you might be very confused. In your mind you know that none of this is the baby's fault. Yet, you can't help thinking that if the baby never existed you never would have had to have the abortion. Anger towards your baby doesn't last long. It is usually replaced quickly with tender feelings for your baby.

You may be angry with yourself for becoming pregnant, for letting your parents down, or for not loving your baby more. You know why you are angry with yourself. It is very important to be aware of these angry feelings toward yourself. If these feelings are denied you may harm yourself without knowing why. Try to realize that most young girls have abortions because of intense fears and pressures. No one really wants to have an abortion. More than likely they feel it is their only choice under the circumstances. Very seldom do teens have abortions for purely selfish reasons.

"I know I wouldn't have been a good mother. I would have felt sorry for my baby. I wanted to have fun. I wanted to go to college. When I see other girls laughing and playing with their babies I have to look away. Working, going to school, and raising a baby is hard for them, but their babies are alive and mine isn't. Why wasn't I strong enough? I know my mom would have helped."

"It hurt to even hear the word adoption. I thought I could never carry a baby for that long and then just give it away. My friends would have thought I was terrible. Abortion was the only choice for me. Annie, my best friend, and I were pregnant at the same time, but we didn't know it. When I found out she was making an adoption plan for her baby, I thought, "How could she?" Annie cries a lot because she misses Joey. That's the name the adoptive parents gave the baby. But Annie gets pictures of Joey and letters from his parents. I don't have anything."

"I didn't believe in abortion and I didn't want an abortion. There just wasn't any way I could tell my parents I was pregnant. I was raped and I was afraid I would hate the baby. Now I wish I had told them. I know they would have been angry with me for being so stupid and for being where I shouldn't have been, but they would have stopped me from having the abortion. I chose to end my baby's life because I didn't like how it was made. I'm mad 'cause I didn't deserve to be raped and my baby didn't deserve to die. I feel as bad as the man who raped me."

Expressing your anger. Many people are afraid of their anger. This is because they think that anger is wrong. Anger is not wrong. It is a feeling. Handling your anger is another thing. You can choose to express your anger in a good or a bad way. Hurting yourself or someone else because of anger is never right. Taking anger out on yourself by refusing to eat or abusing drugs doesn't make your anger go away. Yelling or using violence against those who hurt you will only make matters worse and can never be undone. It will leave you feeling guilty. Violence can destroy a relationship forever.

You can begin to manage your anger by naming everyone you are angry with. Under each name write why you are angry with them. Then write a letter to each and every one of them. You do not have to send or mail these letters. Airing your anger in this way is safe. You will not be shouted at. You can say all you have to say and not be interrupted. Most importantly, writing these letters will help you to understand yourself. Be clear, specific and honest. No one is going to read these letters except for you. Write them in your journal or notebook. If you decide to give these letters to someone be prepared for a reaction. Don't use foul language or swear words. Use words that describe how you really feel. Some samples are given here.

Dear Mama,

You made all my decisions for me. You said you knew what was best for me, but you didn't. I haven't felt the same since I had my abortion. When you took me to the abortion clinic you took away my right to make my own decision. You took away my baby's right to live. Now I'm the one who has to live with this. Do you really love me? Did you care about how it felt? Didn't you think I loved my baby? Every day I think about my baby, but no one is sad about it but me. I will get through this and I will become stronger. I am going to do everything I can to help myself.

Hurting because of you,
Iesha

Dear Craig,

I keep thinking about the day I told you I was pregnant. You were so kind and gentle and told me I could do whatever I wanted. I should have been more honest with you. I wanted to scream at you and ask you, "Why don't you beg me to save your child?". Our baby was created out of our love, but it wasn't love that ended it's life. Where was the man in you who was supposed to protect his child? Why didn't you offer to help support and raise the baby instead of offering to pay for an abortion? Unless we get some kind of help, I don't think I can ever love you again?

In pain,
Celine

If you are creative, you can express your anger through a poem or a drawing. When you feel that your anger may get out of control, take some time out for exercise. Put some of that anger and energy into walking or running. Participating in school sports can also help. If you feel like hitting someone or something, try this technique. Take a pillow and punch it in one corner. As you punch the pillow say what you are angry about. Turn the pillow to the next corner, punch it and mention something else that you are angry about. Keep doing this until you think you have spent all your anger.

Sometimes you may feel so much anger, you will think it is impossible to get rid of it. Nothing you try eases the anger. At this time, or any time, ask Jesus to take your anger from you. He will gladly do this, because he wants you to heal. He will make it possible for you to let go of your anger by taking it from you.

Each time you feel angry, you will need to find a way to express it. You will need to use one of these methods or any other method which works for you. You can use these methods to deal with the anger from your abortion as well as in everyday life.

Expressing your anger in proper ways is good. Be careful, however, not to focus so much on your anger that it covers up the grief you are trying to work through.

Bargaining

When we say we got a real bargain, we mean that we think we made a real good deal. In the case of abortion, a baby's life has been traded for a career, freedom from the expense of raising a child, or keeping the love of those who are close to us. The post-abortive woman often decides that she doesn't like the deal she made. She thinks she paid too high a price, so she tries to make a better deal.

You may not even know that you are trying to make a new bargain. Many girls throw themselves into their studies. They think that if they work hard enough, the sacrifice of having an abortion will have been worth it. Some girls give all their time to the church and others become devoted to their parents. Other young women put in endless hours working for a good cause. Those who already have children try to become supermoms. All of these actions are admirable, but they cannot undo your abortion or bring back your baby. It is right to do good works, but these good works cannot take the place of working through grief and making peace with God.

Your arms may ache from wanting to hold a baby. Sometimes it helps to hold a teddy bear or a doll.

Having an "atonement" baby. Teen mothers often become pregnant again soon after having an abortion, especially if they were forced into it. Your sorrow may be so deep that the only thing you can think of to comfort yourself is to have another baby. Your arms may actually ache from wanting to hold a baby. Many young moms become pregnant again, so God will forgive them, but God will forgive you anyway. Counselors who work with teens after abortion loss know that repeat pregnancy will not ease your grief. A repeat pregnancy will not make you happy. Hearing the baby's heartbeat, seeing the baby on an ultrasound, or feeling the baby move will make you more aware of the life of your aborted baby. If you haven't resolved your grief and experienced complete forgiveness, you will not be best prepared to raise a child. Many teen mothers are surprised to find that they feel depressed after having a second, much wanted baby. They begin to realize that this baby nor any other baby can ever replace the aborted child. They begin to wonder again where the aborted baby is and what their child might have grown up to be.

"Approximately one in three women who have had an abortion try to become pregnant again specifically to replace the child they lost in their abortion. About 18 percent of women who abort actually become pregnant within one year of their abortion."[33] Many young girls want to become pregnant in order to make up for the abortion. Young fathers often try to resolve their grief by talking the teen mother into having another baby. This is because young fathers have little emotional support and are unable to talk about their grief. Young mothers think, "If I become pregnant again, I'll have a chance to do it right this time." The problem with this bargain is that teenagers usually find themselves facing the same pressures to abort that they had with their first pregnancy. They still want to finish school, parents may still be in control and force them to have another abortion, or the baby's father is still not in a position to support and care for them. This is how a cycle of repeat abortions can begin. Repeating abortions over and over again is a form of self punishment. You can keep yourself in a constant state of pain. Please, remember God loves you and does not want you to suffer any more.

There are many important reasons to delay having another baby. Having one pregnancy right after another can place you and your baby at great risk for health problems. Your body needs time to heal. It has to replace the nutrients lost from pregnancy, surgery, and stress. Your body is still growing and needs all the vitamins and nutrients that you take in. If you become pregnant again, your baby will have to compete with you for these nutrients. It is not true that a baby gets what it needs first. Women who wait until they are twenty years old to have a baby have healthier children. Their babies are less likely to be born too early, too small, or to die. Waiting also gives you time to get yourself in the best shape possible. You can form healthy eating patterns, lose or gain weight if needed, and get in the habit of taking daily vitamins. There will be time to quit smoking. If you use drugs or alcohol to dull your pain, there is time to enter and complete a program that will teach you better ways to cope.

Besides giving yourself time to be in good physical shape, you need time for your hurts to heal. Sometimes girls become pregnant to replace the love they lost through the death, divorce, or desertion of someone they loved. Some become pregnant to escape a home in which they are physically or sexually abused. Others become pregnant because they don't do well in school and have few friends. It is not fair to expect a little baby to solve such big problems. Problems just don't go away and having a baby won't make things better. Learning how to love and care for yourself will. You can't love and take care of a baby unless you know how to do this for yourself first. This means asking a school counselor, social worker, or clergyperson for guidance. They can direct you to grief, substance abuse, physical abuse, and sexual abuse support groups. They will be able to help you find a safer place to live and get the counseling that you need, as well as arrange testing for learning disabilities. When you heal your hurts, solve your problems, and let go of your anger, you lessen the risk of abusing a baby.

A lack of money causes a lot of stress for teenage parents. Without a good income, it is hard to find a safe, clean, place to live, get good medical care, and provide for the extras that a baby might need. By completing your education, you will be able to provide what your child needs. Babies born to young parents with little education are poor, don't do as well in school, and have more behavior problems. Postponing pregnancy will also give you a chance to learn good parenting skills.

Now is a good time to think about abstinence and secondary virginity. Secondary virginity is when young people decide to stop having sex until after they are married. Many young people have second thoughts about having sex after an abortion, a pregnancy, or the end of a relationship. When a person is sexually active they have to worry about pregnancy and sexually transmitted diseases. A young woman who has sex with too many partners is more likely to get cervical cancer. This is the opening of the uterus or womb where a baby grows. Secondary virginity will free you from that worry.

Young people have many other reasons for choosing secondary virginity.

"I just don't want to be used any more."

"When I get married, I don't want to have to tell my spouse that I had

"Sometimes it takes a painful experience to make us change our ways."
Proverbs 20:30

sex with ten, twenty, or thirty other people."

"I didn't like myself when I was sexually active. I felt cheap and dirty."

"My girlfriend and I had so much sex we didn't talk or really get to know one another."

"I want someone to love me for who I am, for my thoughts, my ideas, my plans."

"I got pregnant once, he left me, and I said I was never going to make the same mistake again."

There is another big bonus to secondary virginity. Your relationships will be built on true love and not sex. You will become friends first, exchange ideas, do fun things together on dates and learn to express love through sharing.

To become a secondary virgin, follow these steps.

1. First, decide that secondary virginity is something you really want for yourself.
2. Second, forgive yourself for past sexual relationships.
3. Third, promise yourself and God that you will live by your decision.
4. Fourth, avoid people, places, drugs, alcohol, or anything else that will influence you to say "yes" instead of "no".
5. Fifth, learn ways to express love without having sex.
6. Sixth, if you slip up, start all over again.

You need time to make peace with God. Many young people are angry with God or afraid of God's anger, so they avoid Him. If you avoid God, you are missing out on the greatest love of all. Often we confuse God's love with the kind of love our parents give us. We forget that God is the perfect parent, that He loves us even with our faults and is always willing to forgive. He is saddened by all you have been through and wants you to know how much He loves you. There isn't any problem that is too small or too big for Him to handle, but you need to learn to ask for His help through prayer. God wants you to get to know Him and His Son, Jesus, personally. He wants you to turn to Him for comfort, forgiveness, and the grace to turn your life around.

> *"Be merciful to me, Lord,*
> *for I am in trouble;*
> *my eyes are tired from so much crying:*
> *I am exhausted by sorrow,*
> *and weeping has shortened my life.*
> *I am weak from all my troubles,*
> *even my bones are wasting away."*
> **Psalm 31: 10,11**

Depression

Feeling down on yourself, sudden and long outbursts of crying, and deep sadness are marks of depression. There is a loss of hope. You do not want to get up or go to school because you cannot concentrate. You don't care what you look like and you don't want boys to notice you anyway. Perhaps you think you will never be able to love again. You can't get a good night's sleep or you sleep too much to forget about your sadness. Nothing tastes good or you want to eat everything in sight to fill the empty feeling inside you.

Depression uses up all your energy. It will be a major effort to get dressed, shower and make your bed. You don't enjoy doing things you used to do. You don't enjoy yourself at parties or with your best friends. The most serious signs of depression are suicidal thoughts. You may feel unworthy and bad. Maybe, you believe you are no good to anyone. Most of all you want to be with your baby. If you have thoughts of suicide, you need help. Thousands of women who have had an abortion are ready and willing to help you. What you need is love, encouragement and support. They want you to know that your life has great value and that they have the strength to get you through this. If you are having suicidal thoughts call one of the organizations listed in the back of the book now!

Depression can occur right after an abortion. This is partly due to a change in hormones. You body will also tell you that you are no longer pregnant. Your morning sickness will go away or you may notice that your breasts are no longer tender.

Sometimes depression appears about six weeks after an abortion. You will realize that your body is not growing with pregnancy and your monthly period will be coming soon if you have not already had one.

The date the baby was due and the anniversary of the abortion are also common times to have feelings of depression. This time can be critical for you. You may be tempted to turn to drugs and alcohol to relieve the pain. Drugs and alcohol are cheap and easy to get, but remember it will take increased amounts to get the same "high" effect. By trying to run away from your grief, you run the risk of becoming an addict. If you become pregnant while using these substances, you also risk the health of your child. A wiser decision would be to avoid drugs and alcohol, especially when you are depressed.

Depression is a normal part of the process of grieving. You have a right to be sad after your loss and crying is a good way to express your grief. Use your journal to write about your feelings of sadness. Share theses feelings about the abortion with others in an abortion recovery group or with a trusted counselor. **However, depression that lasts for more than two weeks at a time, suicidal thoughts, and being dependent on drugs and alcohol to relieve pain are signs that you need professional help right away!**

Acceptance

Once you have named your losses, spent all your anger, realized that bargains can't bring back your baby, and suffered the sadness of depression, you will understand that the only grief work left to do is to accept the loss of your baby. Working through your grief is like taking off a blindfold and cleaning out your ears. You are now able to see and hear the truth about what happened. This gives you the freedom to keep following the path of healing. You have begun your journey with emotional healing but your healing is not yet complete. If you stop here you will be left half and not whole.

"They may look and look,
yet not see:
they may listen and listen,
yet not understand.
For if they did, they would turn to God,
and He would forgive them."
Mark 4:12

Hope

The path of healing leads to the road of hope for a new and better life. You no longer have to bury your feelings, pain, and mistakes. As Jesus rose from the dead, your loving Father in heaven asks you to rise to a new life and bring these things to Him. He wants you to be healed not only of your emotional and physical pain, but of your spiritual pain as well. Spiritual pain is caused by being separated from your Father in heaven. He wants you to be reunited with Him. This is done through forgiveness.

"Forgiveness brings a hope for a new life."

Happy are those whose sins
are forgiven,
whose wrongs are pardoned.
Psalm 32:1

CHAPTER NINE

Forgiveness

Many of us are very willing to go to a counselor or a doctor for emotional and physical healing. Spiritual healing is another thing. This is when we stop short, and what usually stops us is fear. If you want to stop at this point, you won't be the first person to ever feel this way. However, by stopping now you will either enter a cycle of hurting and punishing yourself again or prevent yourself from receiving complete healing.

This chapter describes the experience of forgiveness in Christianity. If you belong to one of the many other world religions, you may feel more comfortable asking your own spiritual leader for help or reading your own holy book. No matter what religion you practice, you are warmly invited to read this chapter.

The thought that we have caused pain and heartache to those we love is unbearable. *Why are we so afraid to talk about forgiveness?* We are afraid of the worst that could ever happen to us. We are afraid that we will not be forgiven. We are afraid that we will be parted from God and from those we love forever. Another thing that stops us from asking for forgiveness is that we have to admit that we did something wrong. We have to admit that we hurt God, ourselves, the baby, and others who are close to us. The thought that we have caused pain and heartache to those we love is unbearable. Often we avoid these sad thoughts by not forgiving others. If we focus on how others have hurt us, then we do not have to admit that we have hurt anyone.

The truth is that forgiveness is blessed, wonderful, and joyous. It heals the wounds that people have caused each other. It brings you back into the arms of those you love. Forgiveness frees you from guilt and from having to blame others for your actions. It releases you from the past so you can start a new life. It brings lasting peace. Forgiveness is a promise given by God and is yours for the asking.

You do not have to earn your forgiveness. You do not have to punish yourself or make yourself suffer. You may have tried to earn your forgiveness by becoming pregnant again and raising the baby, by being the perfect student, by volunteering your time, or working extra hard at your job. Perhaps you are trying to be the perfect son or daughter, boyfriend, girlfriend, or spouse. None of these things can earn forgiveness. Your forgiveness was earned two thousand years ago, not by you, but by Jesus. It is up to you to accept it.

Before you began grieving for your baby, your emotions were overflowing. Now that you have grieved for your baby and let your tears spill, there is an empty place in you that needs to be filled. God means for that place to be filled with the inflowing of His mercy and a new love and personal relationship with His Son, Jesus.

When Jesus lived on this earth, He taught, He healed, and He forgave sins. When He died, He made up for our sins. When He arose from the dead, He gave us hope for new life. This is God's plan for health and happiness which He means to share with us for all eternity.

Jesus asks us to love one another. That's because love heals our emotional problems. Jesus heals those who asked to be healed. Through prayer, we can ask Jesus to heal our bodies of pain and disease. Jesus forgives sins and forgives us every time we confess our sins. Forgiveness heals our souls. God made us with a body, a mind, and a soul. That is why when we ask to be healed it must be wholly and completely, body, mind, and soul.

Forgiving God

You may be telling yourself you don't have any right to be angry with God. At the same time you know that deep in your heart you are very angry with Him. Perhaps you are angry with Him for letting you get pregnant in the first place. Maybe you think God should have changed the heart of your boyfriend so he would marry you or fix his finances so he could marry you.

God loves us and He doesn't put limits on His love. His perfect love comes with the gift of free will. We are free to choose how we will act and what we will do. We often forget that in our choosing we are refusing God's love. This story might explain it better:

A young girl went to the drugstore to buy some lipstick. While she was there she thought she discovered how to steal the lipstick without getting caught. However, she did get caught. After she told me this, she asked, "Why did God let me get caught? I've been good. I've never stolen anything before. Just this once couldn't He have let me get away with it?" I told her that God didn't let her get away with stealing the lipstick because He loved her and not because He didn't love her. He wanted to keep her close to Him. If God had let her get away with stealing the lipstick she would have hung on to her guilt. Hidden guilt keeps us away from God. She may have continued to steal and feel even more guilty. Since she would be carrying all this guilt she may have felt unworthy to go to church. She may have stopped praying and talking with God. Sometimes God does let us get away with something hoping that we will see the error of our ways. Our own parents often do the same, but there comes a point when our parents and God feel they have to step in to prevent us from doing any more harm to ourselves and others.

> *"My son, pay attention when the Lord corrects you,*
> *and do not be discouraged when He rebukes you.*
> *Because the Lord corrects everyone He loves, and punishes*
> *everyone He accepts as a son."*
> **Hebrews 12:5,6**

Death is something that a lot of people are angry with God about. We often blame God for death. Johnny may have died in an accident but we fail to see that he chose to speed around that bend. Mario was fatally shot but we overlook the fact that he decided to be in a gang. Dad had heart disease but he still smoked. With abortion, your thoughts may be, "If God didn't let me get pregnant, I wouldn't have had to end my baby's life." Even if you were forced to have an abortion against your will, you must understand and accept the responsibility for choosing to be sexually active so that pregnancy was a possibility. If your pregnancy was a result of rape or sexual abuse then you cannot be blamed for the pregnancy, but you did choose to end the baby's life.

Since we are human and we do not think like God, it takes us a longer time to see that our suffering does not mean that God doesn't love us. God would never hurt any of His children. The bad things that happen to us come from satan. God turns our suffering into something of great value. That special something is a closer relationship with Him. God already knows everything about us and loves us completely. It is we who do not know all about God and withdraw our love from Him. Through our suffering we learn to know and love God. We go back to the arms of our Father in heaven who comforts us.

Being angry is a normal emotion and being angry with God is a common human experience. Still we are afraid of this emotion because we think it is wrong, so we deny it. Maybe it's because we are afraid of what we will do with that anger. The truth is that if we do not question God, we will not become as close to Him as we possibly can.

So, what is the best way to handle our anger at God? First, be honest with God. No relationship can be a close one unless it is an honest one. Moses was very outspoken when he talked to God, at one point saying, "If you are going to treat me like this, have pity on me and kill me, so that I won't have to endure your cruelty any longer." (Numbers 11:14,15) Like Moses, you, too, can be honest with God. God can take your anger because He understands it.

Secondly, make up with God as soon as possible. This can be done through a simple prayer like this:

"Dear God, You know I am angry with you for _____.
I have been thinking about You a lot lately and I have decided I don't understand You. Please help me to know and understand You better and to let go of this anger. In the meantime, I want to make peace with You. I realize that all the bad that has happened to me does not come from You. I do not blame You for the abortion because I know that isn't what You wanted. Thank You for loving me."

Once you have admitted your anger and made peace with God, go on to forgiving others and yourself. If you find yourself becoming angry with God again, just admit it and make peace with Him again. This may happen every day or once a year, but don't stay away from God because of your anger.

Forgiving Others

Why is it so important for you to forgive others? Forgiving others will keep you healthier. You will have fewer headaches, stomach aches, and other symptoms. Your energy will increase because you won't have to spend any more energy being angry. Bitterness and hate get in the way of loving and being loved. Forgiving others will help you to let go of the abortion, the pain, and the past. It will help you to forgive yourself. What is most important, is that forgiving others frees you to ask for forgiveness from God.

Our ideas about forgiveness are often confused. We do not know what forgiveness means or how to go about it. The expression "forgive and forget" has led us to have some false ideas about forgiving.

Forgiving does not mean forgetting. We need to remember so we will not let these hurts happen again. Forgiving does not mean making excuses for someone either. Sometimes it helps to understand why they did what they did, but each of us must still be responsible for what we have done. It isn't an easy thing to forgive someone who has hurt us. It's even harder to forgive someone who won't say they are sorry.

59

Forgiveness is a choice and a decision. In order for us to truly forgive others, we must do so with our own free will. We must decide that we want to forgive or at least learn how to forgive. If we are told by someone to say I'm sorry, or if we pretend to forgive someone, or even if we try to forgive because God wants it that way, true forgiveness will not take place. We will not know the true freedom of forgiveness. We will not feel that weight lifted from our shoulders.

In order to forgive, we have to face the pain that others have caused us. This is a good time to take out the letters that you wrote to those you are or were angry with. At this point you can choose to hold on to your anger or to let it go. What you should know is that holding on to your anger is a big load. It weighs you down. Sometimes we get tired of being angry with everyone and we really want to forgive but somehow just can't do it. **It helps to remember that forgiveness is a decision and not a feeling that comes over us.** It might be impossible to forgive without God's help. Give your anger to God. Let God deal with those who have hurt you. This will open a door for God to work with you and teach you how to forgive.

Another thought that sometimes helps is knowing that if we do not forgive others, they are not free to be forgiven. "If you forgive people's sins, they are forgiven; if you do not forgive them, they are not forgiven." Matthew 6:14 Most of us do not want to be guilty of holding someone bound to their sins and not releasing them to God for forgiveness.

Every time we say the Lord's Prayer, we ask to be forgiven as we forgive others. This is why Mother Theresa wrote in The Brotherhood of Man, "It is by forgiving that one is forgiven." In Luke 6:37, he tells us that Jesus said, "Do not judge others, and God will not judge you; do not condemn others, and God will not condemn you; forgive others and God will forgive you." In a letter to the Ephesians 4:31,32, Paul wrote, "Get rid of all bitterness, passion, and anger. No more shouting or insults, no more hateful feelings of any sort. Instead be kind to one another, and forgive one another, as God has forgiven you through Christ." Lastly, say the words of Jesus as he was being crucified. "Forgive them, Father! They don't know what they are doing." (Luke 23:34)

Asking God to Forgive You

"This is a true saying to be completely accepted and believed: Christ Jesus came into the world to save sinners. I am the worst of them, but God was merciful to me in order that Christ Jesus might show his full patience in dealing with me, the worst of sinners, as an example for all those who would later believe in him and receive eternal life." A letter from Paul to Timothy 1:15

Like Paul, many of us think we are "the worst of sinners". We think that we are so bad that God cannot possibly forgive us for what we have done. When we think about facing God with all our sins, we have a picture of an angry, unforgiving God. This is probably the way we think of our earthly parents. We have forgotten that God is the perfect parent, all loving and all forgiving. We forget that God loves us even when we disobey Him. Replace this picture with a heavenly Father who is waiting to welcome you into His open arms, filled with joy knowing that you are sorry. Then realize that not only has God forgiven you, but He celebrates by giving you the gift of eternal life to share and be happy with Him forever in heaven.

Tommy's Story

One day, eight year old Tommy sneaked out to the garage to borrow his dad's tools to build a ramp for roller blading but didn't put them back. When Tommy's dad went to get his tools to do some repairs around the house, he found they were missing. Tommy's dad began to rant and rave saying he knew it was Tommy that took them. "That's it! I've had it with that kid. When I find him, he'll be grounded to his room for a week."

Tommy stood shaking, hidden in his room, where his father hadn't looked for him yet. Tommy knew he broke one of his dad's rules: "Never take my tools without asking and when you do, put them back as soon as you are through using them." Knowing his dad was angry with him, he also knew he had to face him sooner or later. Tommy gathered up his courage to approach his dad, because he also knew his dad loved him. Tommy's dad had sacrificed a lot for his family, although Tommy was too young to understand this. Tommy only knew that his dad worked hard to take care of him and give him what he needed.

Slowly Tommy walked down the hall to find his dad. He stood before him with his head bowed and tears in his eyes. "I'm sorry, dad. I took your tools and forgot to put them back. I promise I won't do it again." In a very harsh tone his dad said, "Tommy, I've asked you again and again and again not to take my tools without asking and to put them back when you're through with them." Hearing this, Tommy began to cry harder. "I know, dad. I didn't listen to you, again. I keep trying to remember." Tommy's dad could see that he was truly sorry and his heart began to soften. "Okay, son, we'll give it another shot. I'll forget about it this time if you clean the tools and put them back right now." Then he gave Tommy a big hug and told him he loved him.

Like Tommy, you, too, know that you have disobeyed the Father and that He is angry with you. At the same time, you are feeling so bad about yourself that you think your Father couldn't possibly love you or forgive you. You may even be thinking that the Father could love and forgive everyone but you. Yet, you want to be loved by God and you want to be forgiven so everything will be right between you and your Father again.

It will take a lot of courage to admit that you are wrong, but you also know that it is the only way to make things right again. Take that first step, knowing that God loves you. In fact God loves you so much "that he gave his only Son, so that everyone who believes in him may not die but have eternal life. For God did not send his Son into the world to be its judge, but to be its Savior." (John 3:16,17) You are God's child and He sacrificed His Son to make up for your sins. You may not fully know what this sacrifice means. You may be spiritually young and you just don't understand it. What you do know is that you won't feel right until your Father forgives you.

So bravely confess your abortion to God, say I'm sorry, clean up your act, and promise never to do it again. This is all your Father asks. If you are one of many young girls who have had a repeat abortion, take heart in knowing that your Father will forgive you again and again and again.

Forgiving Yourself

"I'll never forgive myself," Jamila said sobbing. "I can never forget what I did." If you are thinking like Jamila, you are still judging yourself. God has said that your sins "are no more," but you are still accusing yourself. When God has forgiven you, your baby has forgiven you, and you have forgiven others, nothing should stand in the way of forgiving yourself. The only one who wants you to think this way, is satan. Don't be fooled by him.

"I'll never forgive myself. I can never forget what I did." If you are still thinking like this, you are still judging yourself.

When you don't forgive yourself, you condemn yourself to a life in which you will keep on punishing yourself. You have suffered enough. God wants you to be happy. As you forgave others, make a firm decision to forgive yourself. Then do it. Say, "I'm sorry I did this to myself. I'm not going to let this happen again. I will accept God's love and take care of myself the way He wants me to. "You will then be free to start a whole new peaceful life.

Asking Your Baby to Forgive You

"Where is my baby now?", "Will my baby know me in Heaven?", and "Will my baby forgive me?" are troubling questions that young parents of aborted babies ask. Your baby is being cared for by God, Our Father. Our Father wants all children and their parents to come together in heaven and be happy with Him there. Your baby will be waiting for you. Since your baby has been cared for by the Father, your baby knows how to forgive. Your baby doesn't even know that there is such a thing as not forgiving.

No One Told Me I Could Cry

If you have not given your baby a name, this is the time to do so. The place in your heart that carries the painful word "abortion" is then filled with your baby's name. It is time to let your baby go now. This is the final step of healing. It is called closure. Written on the following page is an exercise to help you do this. Say your baby's name whenever you see a blank. You can read it through first and then pick a good time and place for you to do this. Give yourself plenty of time. Don't rush it. This is your time with your baby.

Picture what _____ looks like. You now know in your heart that you are a parent to a real, living, beautiful baby. _____ is not living with you, but is happy living with his Father in heaven. Now, close your eyes for a moment and picture Jesus holding _____. Jesus hands _____ to you. Tenderly you take _____ into your arms. Allow yourself time to kiss and hold _____ Tell _____everything you want to and ask _____ to forgive you. It is now time to say good-bye to _____. Doing this is heart-wrenching and painful, but now you give _____ back to the Father to watch over until you are reunited in heaven. Now listen to _____."I forgive you and love you. I will pray for you and all my brothers and sisters that are born and yet to be born. Be happy mommy and daddy." If you have sought forgiveness and have forgiven, and have accepted being saved by Jesus, you no longer have to wish that you will see your baby again. It is a promise and a gift from God the Father.

Since your baby is in heaven and you cannot be with your baby yet, you will probably want to find some way to remember your baby here on this earth. Some parents donate a gift to charity in their child's memory. Others donate toys to poor children at Christmas. You can plant a tree in memory of your baby or place a statue of a baby angel in your home. You can also purchase a plaque with your baby's name on it to be placed at a special memorial site for unborn babies. Take time to find the best way for you to honor and remember your baby.

You will always carry your baby in your heart and you will always have memories of your baby. Tears will continue to come. These tears are called "bittersweet." They are tears of sadness and joy, because you have suffered the loss of your baby, but it is your baby who led you to God and His peace.

*"Fresh as the morning, as
sure as the sunrise.
The Lord is all I have, and
so in Him I put my hope."*
Lamentations 3:22-24

CHAPTER TEN

Hope and Joy

It's time to start living. Unload all your troubles and tears and give them to God. The Holy Spirit can then bring you peace and joy. Rejoice and be happy. You are loved. Christ is alive in you. You are forgiven and because you have been forgiven you can more easily forgive others. Because you have suffered, you will now be more loving and understanding of others. You will want to do what's right. You will want to do things for God and help those who need it. You can look forward to spending eternity with all God's family.

From this point on, no matter what situation you are in, there will always be hope. This hope comes through the risen Christ and forgiveness.

Future Plans and Goals

Imagine that you are an artist and a pure, blank canvas is sitting on your easel. On it you will paint your future. Don't let anyone else tell you what to paint on that canvas. The best counsel for your future will come from God. Pray about what you want to do with the rest of your life. Make drawings, paintings or etchings of yourself in the future. What will you be doing one year from now? Two years from now? Five or ten years from now? If you can't draw then write. Do you want to go to college? Do you see yourself in a business suit? Do you see yourself with your own home, a husband, and a family?

It is often said that our dreams are gifts from God. Follow your dreams and use the talents God gave you to form goals and make plans for the future. For example, if God blessed you with a beautiful voice and you would like to sing, you can set these goals for yourself. Your first goal can be to sing in the church choir or school chorus. Your second goal can be to try out for a part in the school musical. Your third goal can be to arrange for voice lessons that you can afford or a music teacher to be your mentor. Your fourth goal can be to look into colleges that will train you to be a music teacher yourself. Don't hold yourself back. God wants you to be happy!

Maybe for now your goal is to be healed of an addiction. The goals you can set for yourself are to find an addictions counselor or to enter a rehab program. Maybe you would just like to learn how to cope with an alcoholic parent. Set a goal to join Alateen so you will have support from other teens living with alcoholic parents. The point is that all things are possible with God and this gives you the power to change your life. Allow God to change your hopelessness and depression into hope and joy. Take it one day at a time. Accept the love of the Father, the forgiveness of Jesus, the guidance of the Holy Spirit and the support of thousands of other people in this world who have suffered, found God, and now want to help you.

Celebrate by thanking God!

"You have changed my sadness into a joyful dance;
you have taken away my sorrow
and surrounded me with joy.
So, I will not be silent;
I will sing praise to you.
Lord, you are my God;
I will give you thanks forever."
Psalm 30:11,12

Where To Get Help

There are many people and places willing to help after abortion. You have a lot of choices. Some refer to counselors and clergy that have been trained for post-abortion counseling. Some offer group support. Others offer workbooks. There are men only and women only agencies as well as agencies that offer support for both men and women. A few organizations are located on the Internet. Most are able to support those in any religion, and some are not religiously based but will offer assistance in spiritual counseling when you are ready. Please read through this entire list to see which contacts will best help you.

Post-Abortion Ministries

Care Net
109 Carpenter Drive
Sterling, VA 20164
Toll free phone number: 800-395-HELP

Care Net is associated with over 400 crisis pregnancy centers and plans on opening 35 more centers each year. Their postabortion workbook for women is Forgiven and Set Free. Their workbook for men is called Healing a Father's Heart. Call their toll free number to be connected to the crisis pregnancy center nearest you.

Heartbeat International
7870 Olentangy River Road, Suite 304
Columbus, OH 43235-1319
Phone 614-885-7577

Heartbeat centers offer support to people who are experiencing or have experienced problem pregnancies. Services include post-abortion counseling and group support at over 350 crisis pregnancy centers in 46 states and 10 foreign countries. A workbook HEART: *Healing the Effects of Abortion Related Trauma* is also available.

Last Harvest Ministries/HopeNet
2722 W. Kingsley Road Suite 112
Garland, TX 75041
Toll free phone number: 888-HOPE-4-ME
E-Mail address: hopenet@flash.net
Web Site: http://www.flash.net/~hopenet

This is a Christian based organization that offers personal telephone and E-mail help. They can also refer you to a church or crisis pregnancy center that can offer group support. A post-abortion workbook *Healing the Hurt of Abortion* is available for both men and women at low cost. A recovery workbook for healing other hurts in your life is also available. Assistance in finding legal aid, adoption agencies, and maternity homes are some of the many other services they provide.

The National Office of Post-Abortion Reconciliation and
Healing (N.O.P.A.R.H.)
3501 South Lake Drive
P.O. Box 07477
Milwaukee, WI 53207-0477
Toll free phone number: 800-5WE-CARE

The National Office of Post-Abortion Reconciliation and Healing can make referrals to women, men, teens, and members of their families of all faiths. Books, tapes, and articles on post-abortion aftermath and healing are available. They can refer you to the nearest church based post-abortion healing ministry, crisis pregnancy center, or Project Rachel (a post-abortion healing ministry for Catholics) in your archdiocese.

Their national post-abortion support referral number is 800-5WE-CARE. Office hours are Monday, Wednesday, and Friday, 9 A.M. to 4 P.M. Central Standard Time.

Open Arms
P.O. Box 9292
Colorado Springs, CO 80932-9292
Phone: 719-573-5790

Open Arms has a catalog of resources on post-abortion materials. Both men and women are invited to participate in their post-abortion Bible study program entitled in *In His Image* which can be worked on individually at home or in a group.

Victims of Choice
P.O. Box 815
Naperville, IL 60560
Phone: 630-378-1680

Victims of Choice offers a post-abortion healing program for both men and women. Lay counselors provide free services and are available across the country and in 9 foreign countries. This is a Christian based program. Call the number above for the counselor nearest you.

Wisconsin Evangelical Lutheran Synod
2401 N. Mayfair Road, Suite 300
Milwaukee, WI 53226-1401
Toll Free Number: 800-729-9535

Provides counseling and referrals and is associated with 24 Lutheran centers.

Internet Counseling

Heart to Heart Ministries
Web Site: http://www.web-light.com/heart/htoho2.htm
E-Mail: htohhdqs@aol.com

Heart to Heart provides one to one e-mail and support group counseling to anyone suffering from the effects of an abortion.

Women In Transition
Phone: 713-968-9097
E-mail: info@wits.org
Web Site: http://www.wits.org

Women In Transition invites you to join their non-denominational, nonjudgmental atmosphere. Women in Transition provides a safe place for women to talk with one another in anonymity about their past abortions. If you are struggling with the after effects of abortion, phone them to speak in confidence to a group leader, or e-mail them for nonjudgmental, compassionate listening and counseling and to learn more about their unique program.

For Men Only

Fathers & Brothers Ministries
350 Broadway, Suite 40
Boulder, CO 80303
Phone: 303-494-3282

The director, Warren L. Williams works with post-abortive men. In addition he has written two publications. They are *Restoration From the Wounds of Lost Fatherhood and Abandonment by Abortion: How Abortion Affects Fathers and How They Can Recover* and *The Ancient Secret of Blessing Your Losses: A Bible Study for Men.*

Men's Abortion ReCovery (MARC Ministries)
Wayne F. Brauning/Director
237 S 13th Avenue
Coatesville, PA 19320
Phone: 610-384-3210

MARC is headed by Wayne Brauning, a Doctor of Ministry, who works with post-abortive men. Four low cost, easy to read, comforting booklets are available. They are *Men and Abortion: The Big Picture, Men and Abortion: What Men Experience, Men and Abortion: the Sexual Dimension, and Men and Abortion: God's Solution.*

If Your Pregnancy Was a Result of Sexual Abuse or Rape

Fortress International
P.O. Box 2562
South Bend, IN 46680-2526
Phone: 219-288-3688

Fortress International was founded by Julie Hakimaa as a prolife education and advice organization for victims of sexual assault and their children. Members are 1) women who have become pregnant as a result of rape or incest and either carried their children to term or had an abortion which they now regret, and 2) juvenile and adult children conceived by sexual assault.

Hotlines

America's Crisis Pregnancy Helpline
Toll free number: 800-67-BABY-6

Provides counseling, information and referrals 24 hours a day.

National Life Center
Toll Free Number: 800-848-LOVE

National Life Center's 24 hour hotline directs you to the closest Crisis Pregnancy Center in the United States and Canada.

Memorial Sites

National Memorial for the Unborn
6230 Vance Road
Chatanooga, TN 37421
Toll free number: 800-505-5565

A fifty foot granite wall is dedicated for remembrance plaques. Mothers and families who have lost unborn children to abortion are encouraged to place plaques on this wall. Plaques may include the name of an unborn child, a special message or reference, and a date. Call or write for information on placing a plaque.

Additional Post-abortion Reading Materials for Men and Women are Available From:

Life Cycle Books
www.lifecyclebooks.com
e-mail: orders@lifecyclebooks.com
Phone: (800) 214-5849
Fax: (888) 690-8532

REFERENCES

1   Doka, KJ. (Ed). (1987). *Recognizing Hidden Sorrow.* Lexington MA: Lexington Books.

2   Warden, JW. (1982). *Grief Counseling and Grief Therapy: A Handbook for the Mental Health Practitioner.* New York: Springer Publishing.

3   Ventura, SJ, Taffel SM, Mosher WD, Wilson JB, Henshaw S. (1995). Trends in pregnancies and pregnancy rates, estimates for the United States, 1980-92. *Monthly Vital Statistics Report,* 43(11) (Suupl).

4   Greydonus, DE., Railsbach, LD. (1985). Abortion in Adolescence. *Seminars in Adolescent Medicine.* 1:213-222.

5   Adler, N. (1975). Emotional response of women following therapeutic abortion. *American Journal of Orthopsychiatry,* 45:446-454.

6   Franz, W., & Reardon, D. (1992). Differential impact of abortion on adolescents and adults. *Adolescence,* 27(105): 1~1-172.

7   Major & Cozzarelli (1992). Psychosocial predictors of adjustment to abortion. *Journal of Social Issues,* 48(3):95-119.

8   Speckhard, C. & Rue V.(1992). Post abortion syndrome: An emerging public health concern. *Journal of Social Issues,* 48(3): 121-142.

9   Smith, EM (1973) A follow-up study of women who request abortion. *American Journal of Orthopsychiatry.* 43:574-585.

10 Somers, R. (1979) *Risk of Admission to Psychiatric Institutions Among Danish Women Who Experienced Induced Abortion: An Analysis Based on National Report Linkage.* Ph. D. Dissertation, Los Angeles: University of California. Dissertation Abstracts International, Public Health 2621 -B Order No. 7926066.

11 Margolis, A., Rindfuss, R., Coghlann, P., & Rochat, R. (1971). Therapeutic abortion: Follow-up study. *American Journal of Obstetrics and Gynecology.* 110:243.

12 Horowitz, NH., (1978). Adolescent mourning reactions to infant and fetal loss. *Social Casework,* 59:351-559.

13 Cvejic, H., Lipper I., Kinch R., & Benjamin P. (1977). Follow-up study of 50 adolescent girls two years after abortion. *Canadian Medical Association Journal* 116:44-46.

14 Amaro, H., Zuckerrnan, B., & Cabral, H. (1989). Drug use among adolescent mothers: Profile of Risk. *Pediatrics,* 84:144-150.

15 Campbell, NB., Flanco, K., & Jurs S. (1988). Abortion in adolescence. *Adolescence,* 23(92):813-823.

16 Ibid.

17 Garfunkel, B., Hoberman, H., Parsons, J., Walker, J. (1986). *Depressions and suicide:* A study of adolescents in Minnesota. Minneapolis: University of MN Extension Service. 78

18 Mieckle, S., Pertchinis, J., & Pearce, K. (1985). *Teenage Sexuality.* San Diego: College-Hill Press.

19 Hatcher, S. (1976). Understanding adolescent pregnancy and abortion. *Primary Care,* 3(3): 407-425.

20 Greydanus, D.E. (1983). In E. R. McAnarney (Ed.), *Premature adolescent pregnancy and parenthood.* (pp. 351-371). New York: Grune & Stratton.

21 Rue, V. (1996). Testimony cited in the effects of abortion on men. *Ethics and Medicine.* 21 :3-4.

22 Redmond, MA.(1985). Attitudes of adolescent males towards pregnancy and fatherhood. *Family Relations,* 34(3): 337-341.

23 Gordon, R.A., & Kilpatrick, C. (1977). A program of group counseling for men accompanying women seeking legal abortions. *Community Mental Health Journal,* 13(4): 291-295.

24 Rothstein, AA. (1978). Adolescent males: fatherhood and abortion. *Journal of Youth and Adolescence,* 7(2): 203-204.

25 Buchanan M., & Robbins, C. (1990). *Consequences of adolescent pregnancy and its resolution as evidenced in adulthood.*

26 Palmer, P. *The Issue of Men and Abortion.* Healing Visions Vll audio tape. Milwaukee, WI: National Office of Post-Abortion Reconciliation and Healing

27 Bell, G., The Issue of Men and Abortion, as quoted by P. Palmer, Healing Visions Vll audiotape. Milwaukee,WI: National Office of Post-Abortion Reconciliation and Healing.

28 Palmer, P. Ibid.

29 Williams, W. *The Issue of Men and Abortion.* Healing Visions Vll audiotape. Milwaukee,WI: National Office of Post-Abortion Reconciliation and Healing.

30 Ibid.

31 Reardon, D. (1996) Forgotten fathers and their unforgettable children. Post Abortion Review, 4(4):3.

32 Crawford, DR., & Mannion, MT. (1989). *Psycho-Spiritual Healing After Abortion.* Kansas City: Sheed & Ward.

33 Reardon, D.C. (1996). *The Jericho plan: Breaking down the walls which prevent post abortion healing.* Springfield, IL: Acorn Books.

Abortion is never easy or painless. But many teens suffer a deep and profound wound after experiencing the loss of a child through abortion. They are often taught to suppress their pain instead of talking about it, and they often don't heal – precisely because they simply don't know how. Connie Nykiel gives teens reason for hope in this wonderful book, by teaching a path to healing for young people. She invites them find new life again – new life in Christ.

Order Directly from Life Cycle Books

Single Copy $13.95 (postpaid)

2 to 9 copies $8.95 each
10 to 49 copies $7.95 each
50 to 99 copies $6.95 each
100 or more copies $6.25 each

For orders on 2 or more books, please add 10% shipping and handling, with a minimum charge of $4.95.

Order from:
LIFE CYCLE BOOKS
P.O. BOX 420
LEWISTON, NY 14092-0420
(800) 214-5849
Please send me _____ copy (ies) of NO ONE TOLD ME I COULD CRY.

Enclosed please find $ _____ to cover the cost of books and shipping

Send book (s) to:

Name: _____

Address: _____

State: _____ Zip _____

Abortion is never easy or painless. But many teens suffer a deep and profound wound after experiencing the loss of a child through abortion. They are often taught to suppress their pain instead of talking about it, and they often don't heal – precisely because they simply don't know how. Connie Nykiel gives teens reason for hope in this wonderful book, by teaching a path to healing for young people. She invites them find new life again – new life in Christ.

Order Directly from Life Cycle Books

Single Copy $13.95 (postpaid)

2 to 9 copies $8.95 each
10 to 49 copies $7.95 each
50 to 99 copies $6.95 each
100 or more copies $6.25 each

For orders on 2 or more books, please add 10% shipping and handling, with a minimum charge of $4.95.

Order from:
LIFE CYCLE BOOKS
P.O. BOX 420
LEWISTON, NY 14092-0420
(800) 214-5849
Please send me _____ copy (ies) of NO ONE TOLD ME I COULD CRY.

Enclosed please find $ _____ to cover the cost of books and shipping

Send book (s) to:

Name: _____

Address: _____

State: _____ Zip _____

Abortion is never easy or painless. But many teens suffer a deep and profound wound after experiencing the loss of a child through abortion. They are often taught to suppress their pain instead of talking about it, and they often don't heal – precisely because they simply don't know how. Connie Nykiel gives teens reason for hope in this wonderful book, by teaching a path to healing for young people. She invites them find new life again – new life in Christ.

Order Directly from Life Cycle Books

Single Copy $13.95 (postpaid)

2 to 9 copies $8.95 each
10 to 49 copies $7.95 each
50 to 99 copies $6.95 each
100 or more copies $6.25 each

For orders on 2 or more books, please add 10% shipping and handling, with a minimum charge of $4.95.

Order from:
LIFE CYCLE BOOKS
P.O. BOX 420
LEWISTON, NY 14092-0420
(800) 214-5849
Please send me _____ copy (ies) of NO ONE TOLD ME I COULD CRY.

Enclosed please find $ _____ to cover the cost of books and shipping

Send book (s) to:

Name: _____

Address: _____

State: _____ Zip _____

Abortion is never easy or painless. But many teens suffer a deep and profound wound after experiencing the loss of a child through abortion. They are often taught to suppress their pain instead of talking about it, and they often don't heal – precisely because they simply don't know how. Connie Nykiel gives teens reason for hope in this wonderful book, by teaching a path to healing for young people. She invites them find new life again – new life in Christ.

Order Directly from Life Cycle Books

Single Copy $13.95 (postpaid)

2 to 9 copies $8.95 each
10 to 49 copies $7.95 each
50 to 99 copies $6.95 each
100 or more copies $6.25 each

For orders on 2 or more books, please add 10% shipping and handling, with a minimum charge of $4.95.

Order from:
LIFE CYCLE BOOKS
P.O. BOX 420
LEWISTON, NY 14092-0420
(800) 214-5849
Please send me _____ copy (ies) of NO ONE TOLD ME I COULD CRY.

Enclosed please find $ _____ to cover the cost of books and shipping

Send book (s) to:

Name: _____

Address: _____

State: _____ Zip _____